PACEMAKER® PRACTICAL ENGLISH SERIES

WRITING MAKES SENSE

Marlene B. Clarke
Arlene G. Clarke

A PACEMAKER® BOOK

Fearon Education
a division of
David S. Lake Publishers
Belmont, California

Pacemaker® Practical English Series

Grammar Makes Sense
Capitalization and Punctuation Make Sense
Writing Makes Sense
Spelling Makes Sense
Vocabulary Makes Sense

ISBN 0–8224–5103–4

Printed in the United States of America

1. 9 8 7 6 5 4 3

CONTENTS

SENTENCES

Complete sentences

If you need help with grammar, capitalization, or punctuation, refer to the Reference Guide on pages 111–123.

A group of words that looks like a sentence but does not have both a subject and a predicate is called a *sentence fragment*.

                Sentence   Sentence fragment

EXAMPLE: *Thebes was a powerful city-state.*   *In Greece.*

Often, a sentence and a sentence fragment can be combined to make one sentence.

EXAMPLE: *Thebes was a powerful city-state in Greece.*

Next to each number below are a complete sentence and a sentence fragment. Combine the groups of words to make a new sentence. You may have to take out or rearrange some words. Write the new sentence on the writing line(s).

1. A man made $2,500,000. By inventing the shoelace.

2. Sand is in many things. Such as bricks and windows.

3. A team once needed 21 runs. To win a baseball game.

4. Ketchup once had a strange use. As a medicine.

5. Ice is hard. About as hard as concrete.

6. A woman had four husbands. Despite her long beard.

7. The average life expectancy for most men was about 35 years. At the time Washington became president.

SENTENCES

Complete sentences

If you need help with grammar, capitalization, or punctuation, refer to the Reference Guide on pages 111–123.

Sometimes you must add to sentence fragments in order to make complete sentences.

Sentence fragment

EXAMPLE: *During the alien invasion.*

Complete sentence

EXAMPLE: *During the alien invasion, I ate popcorn.*

Look at each sentence fragment below, and then add to it to make a complete sentence. Write your new sentence on the writing line.

1. If I were rich.

_____

2. When I'm afraid.

_____

3. Inside the cave.

_____

4. And stayed up all night.

_____

5. To catch a fly.

_____

6. Buried in the yard.

_____

7. Because the TV set was broken.

_____

8. As soon as I saw the envelope.

_____

9. Sneaking around the corner.

_____

SENTENCES

Complete sentences

If you need help with grammar, capitalization, or punctuation, refer to the Reference Guide on pages 111–123.

The paragraph given on the right contains some sentence fragments. Rewrite the paragraph on the lines below. Be sure to make all the sentence fragments into complete sentences.

Buried treasure is everywhere. All over the United States. More than 4 billion dollars' worth. Where did it all come from? Sometimes robbers hid it. But were killed before they could claim it. Pirates and misers also hid their money. Hoping that no one else would find it. Old mines may still contain gold or silver. Some of the most famous mines have not yet been found. Because their owners died without sharing the secret of where the mines were. Often, things that we don't think of as treasure may turn out to be valuable. Like old bottles or old guns that the robbers, misers, and miners left behind. Of course, the question isn't what the treasure is. Or who left it. It's how <u>we</u> can find it.

SENTENCES

Descriptive sentences

If you need help with grammar, capitalization, or punctuation, refer to the Reference Guide on pages 111–123.

Adjectives, adverbs, and prepositional phrases make sentences more vivid and descriptive.

Original sentence

EXAMPLE: *The woman shrieked.*

Improved sentence

The **frightened** woman **in the red dress** shrieked **wildly**.

adjective   prepositional phrase   adverb

Each declarative sentence below is followed by some questions. On the line next to each question, answer the question with an adjective, an adverb, or a prepositional phrase. Then add your answers to the original declarative sentence and write your improved sentence on the writing line.

1. The car leaked oil.

   Was the car battered or brand new? _____

   Did the car leak oil slowly or quickly? _____

   _____

2. The mechanic fixed the leak.

   Was the mechanic cheerful or impatient? _____

   Did the mechanic fix the leak expertly or badly? _____

   Where was the leak? _____

   _____

3. The pitcher hurled the fastball.

   Was the pitcher clumsy or graceful? _____

   How did the pitcher hurl the ball? _____

   Where did the pitcher throw the ball? _____

   _____

   _____

SENTENCES

Descriptive sentences

If you need help with grammar, capitalization, or punctuation, refer to the Reference Guide on pages 111–123.

To each sentence below, add at least one adjective, one adverb, and one prepositional phrase. Write your improved sentence on the writing lines.

1. The bats fluttered.

   _____

   _____

2. The wolves howled.

   _____

   _____

3. The spider crept.

   _____

   _____

4. The coffin lid opened.

   _____

   _____

5. The man turned into a werewolf.

   _____

   _____

6. Dracula appeared.

   _____

   _____

7. The woman fell into the pit of snakes.

   _____

   _____

SENTENCES

Descriptive sentences

If you need help with grammar, capitalization, or punctuation, refer to the Reference Guide on pages 111–123.

Synonyms are words that mean almost the same thing. For instance, *talk* and *speak* are synonyms. But no two words can mean exactly the same thing. Words that have similar meanings can have different effects on the reader or listener. Read the sentences below.

The **secret agent** helped his country by discovering the enemy's plans.

The **spy** carried the secret plans in his trench coat.

The **sneak** crept into the room at night and took pictures of the country's defense plans.

Secret agent, spy, and *sneak* are synonyms. But *secret agent* has a positive effect, *spy* has a neutral effect, and *sneak* has a negative effect.

For each of the following sets of three synonyms, write three sentences on the lines provided. Use the word having a positive effect in the first sentence, the word having a neutral effect in the second sentence, and the word having a negative effect in the third sentence. Use a dictionary if you need help with the meanings of the words.

1. odor   smell   fragrance

_____

_____

_____

2. different   weird   unusual

_____

_____

_____

3. calmly   passively   quietly

_____

_____

_____

4. tell   nag   remind

_____

_____

_____

5. reproduction   fake   copy

_____

_____

_____

6. debate   argue   fight

_____

_____

_____

7. pushy   bold   aggressive

_____

_____

_____

8. miserly   thrifty   economical

_____

_____

_____

9. brimming   full   glutted

_____

_____

_____

SENTENCES

Descriptive sentences

If you need help with grammar, capitalization, or punctuation, refer to the Reference Guide on pages 111–123.

Sentences can be improved by making general words more specific.

Original sentence

EXAMPLE: *I keep my <u>pet</u> on a leash.*

Improved sentence

EXAMPLE: *I keep my **goldfish** on a leash.*

In each sentence below, replace the underlined words with words that are more specific. Write your improved sentence on the writing line.

1. Mr. Spock is <u>an alien</u>.

_____

2. Captain Kirk <u>works on</u> a spaceship.

_____

3. The president <u>eats candy</u>.

_____

4. After eating <u>a snack</u> at midnight, I had a nightmare.

_____

5. <u>Many people</u> waited in line all night for the tickets.

_____

6. A <u>small animal</u> scurried across my room.

_____

7. "I shouldn't have left the scalpel <u>there</u>," the doctor <u>said</u>.

_____

8. "I'll <u>do</u> my book report <u>soon</u>," I promised.

_____

9. <u>The weather was bad</u> during the concert.

_____

SENTENCES

Descriptive sentences

If you need help with grammar, capitalization, or punctuation, refer to the Reference Guide on pages 111–123.

The paragraph given on the right contains many choppy, dull sentences. Rewrite the paragraph on the lines below, making the sentences more vivid and descriptive. Replace general words with ones that are more specific, and add adjectives, adverbs, and prepositional phrases.

It was night. I was lying in bed. I heard a noise. It came from somewhere outside. I got up and looked. I saw a weird light. It came from an odd-shaped vehicle. A door opened. Out came two funny-looking creatures. They were wearing peculiar clothes. Their skin was an unusual color. They spoke to each other in a strange language. I heard more sounds. The two creatures walked across the yard. I heard the door downstairs open and shut. I stayed in bed. I heard footsteps in the house. They got closer. Then I heard a pounding on my door. I woke up and heard my mom. "Time to get up for school!" she called. Aliens never stick around when you need them.

SENTENCES

Compound subjects

If you need help with grammar, capitalization, or punctuation, refer to the Reference Guide on pages 111–123.

Compound subjects can sometimes be used to join short, choppy sentences.

Original sentences

EXAMPLE: *Kangaroos have pouches. So do anteaters.*

Improved sentence

Kangaroos and anteaters have pouches.

Make each pair of sentences below into one sentence by using a compound subject. Write your new sentence on the writing lines.

1. George Washington snored.
   Teddy Roosevelt snored.

   _____

   _____

2. Big Ugly Elementary School is in West Virginia.
   Little Ugly Creek is also in West Virginia.

   _____

   _____

3. Alabama and Georgia have towns called Brooklyn.
   So do Mississippi and South Carolina.

   _____

   _____

4. Kenneth LeBel jumped over 16 barrels on ice skates.
   Jacques Favero did, too.

   _____

   _____

5. Though he wasn't blind, Thomas Edison learned Braille.
   The same was true of Aldous Huxley.

   _____

   _____

SENTENCES

Compound predicates

If you need help with grammar, capitalization, or punctuation, refer to the Reference Guide on pages 111–123.

Compound predicates can sometimes be used to join short, choppy sentences.

Original sentences

EXAMPLE: *Three dolphins rescued a woman thrown from a boat. They also protected her from sharks.*

Improved sentence

Three dolphins rescued a woman thrown from a boat and protected her from sharks.

Make each pair of sentences below into one sentence by using a compound predicate. Write your new sentence on the writing lines.

1. The Australian walking fish can swim and walk.
   It can also climb trees.

   _____

   _____

2. Mark Twain was born when Halley's comet appeared.
   He died when it reappeared.

   _____

   _____

3. A 73-year-old man competed in the 1920 Olympics.
   He won bronze and silver medals in rifle shooting.

   _____

   _____

4. A mosquito has 47 teeth.
   A mosquito can carry twice its own weight.

   _____

   _____

11

SENTENCES

Compound sentences

If you need help with grammar, capitalization, or punctuation, refer to the Reference Guide on pages 111–123.

Sentences can sometimes be improved by the use of coordinating conjunctions to create compound sentences.

Original sentences

EXAMPLE: *Marlon Brando won an Oscar.*
He refused to accept it.

Improved sentence

Marlon Brando won an Oscar, but he refused to accept it.

Make each pair of sentences below into one compound sentence. Use the coordinating conjunction *and, but,* or *or.* Write your new sentence on the writing lines.

1. A lot of people say they like pink soap.
   Pink soap seldom sells very well.

   _____

   _____

2. Roy C. Sullivan was struck by lightning seven times.
   He is still alive.

   _____

   _____

3. Move to Oregon if you want to breathe clean air.
   You can move to Hawaii instead.

   _____

   _____

4. Ninety-one percent of Utah's drivers pump their own gas.
   Only thirty-three percent of the drivers in Maine do.

   _____

   _____

5. King Henry III of France hated cats.
   He fainted if a cat got too close to him.

   _____

   _____

6. Five-year-old Susan Tripp weighed 205 pounds.
   Her three-year-old sister, Deborah, weighed 125 pounds.

   _____

   _____

7. Ants have five noses.
   Each nose does something different.

   _____

   _____

8. Helen Keller was deaf and blind.
   She could identify her friends by their smell.

   _____

   _____

9. Some people believe that the earth is flat.
   Others believe that it is hollow.

   _____

   _____

10. Wilt Chamberlain played 798 hours of pro basketball.
    He never fouled out of a game.

    _____

    _____

11. Boxing matches used to last 100 rounds.
    The boxers wore no gloves.

    _____

    _____

12. In Wyoming, you may want to visit Yellowstone National Park.
    You might prefer to see Grand Teton National Park.

    _____

    _____

SENTENCES

Complex sentences

If you need help with grammar, capitalization, or punctuation, refer to the Reference Guide on pages 111–123.

Sentences can sometimes be improved by the use of subordinating conjunctions to create complex sentences.

Original sentences

EXAMPLE: *Most of us use refrigerators to keep our food cold.*
Alaskans use them to keep their food from freezing.

Improved sentences

While most of us use refrigerators to keep our food cold, Alaskans use them to keep their food from freezing.

and

Most of us use refrigerators to keep our food cold, although Alaskans use them to keep their food from freezing.

Make each pair of sentences below into a complex sentence. Use one of the subordinating conjunctions listed here. Try not to use any conjunction more than once. Write your new sentences on the writing lines.

after	before	though	when
although	if	unless	whenever
because	since	until	while

1. There were no banks in the United States before the Revolution. People had to borrow money from individuals.

   _____

   _____

2. Prisoners escape from a Mexican jail. The guards have to serve out the prisoners' sentences.

   _____

   _____

3. Abraham Lincoln was shot in Ford's Theatre. He was carried across the street to Petersen House, where he died.

   _____

   _____

4. Mount St. Helens erupted in 1980.
   It had been inactive for over 120 years.

   _____

   _____

5. Armstrong and Aldrin landed on the moon in Apollo 11's lunar
   module.
   Collins, the third team member, circled above in the command
   module.

   _____

   _____

   _____

6. Many people have seen the Loch Ness monster.
   No one has ever proved that it exists.

   _____

   _____

7. The president is accompanied by a number of Secret Service
   agents.
   He leaves the White House.

   _____

   _____

8. You're afraid of heights.
   Be sure to go to the top of the Eiffel Tower.

   _____

   _____

9. You can walk across the Mississippi River.
   You cross it at Lake Itasca, Minnesota, where the river begins.

   _____

   _____

10. The polls are closed and the ballots are counted.
    The voters can't know the official results.

    _____

    _____

SENTENCES

Combining and connecting sentences

If you need help with grammar, capitalization, or punctuation, refer to the Reference Guide on pages 111–123.

Make each pair of sentences below into one sentence by following the directions given beneath the pair. You will write either two or three new sentences for each pair given. Write your new sentences on the writing lines.

1. Jeremy Bentham left everything to London Hospital. He said the hospital had to have his corpse present at board meetings.

   A. Form a compound sentence by using a coordinating conjunction.

   _____

   _____

   _____

   B. Form a complex sentence by using a subordinating conjunction.

   _____

   _____

   _____

2. A cat fell from the twentieth floor of a building. It lived.

   A. Form a simple sentence with a compound predicate.

   _____

   _____

   B. Form a compound sentence by using a coordinating conjunction.

   _____

   _____

   C. Form a complex sentence by using a subordinating conjunction.

   _____

   _____

3. It took two weeks for Europeans to hear of Lincoln's assassination. It took only 1.3 seconds for people on Earth to hear that man had landed on the moon.

A. Form a compound sentence by using a coordinating conjunction.

_____

_____

_____

B. Form a complex sentence by using a subordinating conjunction.

_____

_____

_____

4. Bees have their own language.
Whales have their own language.

A. Form a simple sentence with a compound subject.

_____

B. Form a compound sentence by using a coordinating conjunction.

_____

_____

5. A mother dreamed her dead son had been buried alive.
She found out he had been.

A. Form a simple sentence with a compound predicate.

_____

_____

B. Form a compound sentence by using a coordinating conjunction.

_____

_____

C. Form a complex sentence by using a subordinating conjunction.

_____

_____

SENTENCES

Combining and connecting sentences

If you need help with grammar, capitalization, or punctuation, refer to the Reference Guide on pages 111–123.

The paragraph given on the right contains many short, choppy sentences. Rewrite the paragraph on the lines below, combining as many of the short sentences as you can.

Someone takes you out to a restaurant. You expect to have a good time. That's what Mr. Gourier's guests expected. He didn't just entertain them. He killed them. His murder weapon was strange. It was food. The food wasn't poisoned. He took his guests out to eat time after time. The food was heavy and rich. The guests ate too much of it. Their overeating killed them. Some guests died after two months. Others died after a year. Finally, Mr. Gourier's weapon was turned against him. One of his guests said he could eat more than Mr. Gourier could eat. They tried to outdo each other. Mr. Gourier lost. He ate 14 steaks. He died. This time, his guest had to pay the bill.

SENTENCES

Separating run-on sentences

If you need help with grammar, capitalization, or punctuation, refer to the Reference Guide on pages 111–123.

A run-on sentence incorrectly contains two or more sentences. This kind of sentence should be split into separate sentences.

Run-on sentence

EXAMPLE: *Birds eat a lot each year, they eat more than 90 times their own weight in food.*

Correctly separated sentence

Birds eat a lot. Each year, they eat more than 90 times their own weight in food.

Correct each of the following run-on sentences. Write your new sentences on the writing lines.

1. Winston Churchill was born in the cloakroom of a castle his mother was attending a dance.

_____

_____

2. Doris Day's real name is Doris von Kappelhoff Tina Turner's real name is Annie Mae Bullock.

_____

_____

3. Snails produce a thick protective slime they can walk on razor blades without getting cut.

_____

_____

4. It is so cold in Siberia that a person's breath can freeze it falls to the ground and cracks.

_____

_____

SENTENCES

Separating run-on sentences

If you need help with grammar, capitalization, or punctuation, refer to the Reference Guide on pages 111–123.

The paragraph given on the right contains many run-on sentences. Rewrite the paragraph on the lines below, correcting any run-on sentences you find.

There once was a man who really vanished into thin air in 1880, a farmer in Tennessee was walking across a field some of his friends were watching him all of a sudden, the man disappeared thinking he had fallen into a hole, the farmer's friends ran to find him when they got to the spot where he had been, however, they could find neither the man nor a hole the farmer never returned in the place where he had disappeared, the grass grew especially long the farm animals, though, wouldn't eat the grass that grew there.

_____

_____

_____

_____

_____

_____

_____

_____

_____

_____

_____

_____

_____

SENTENCES

Avoiding repetition

If you need help with grammar, capitalization, or punctuation, refer to the Reference Guide on pages 111–123.

Sentences sometimes contain words that repeat information. The repetitous words are not needed and should be taken out.

Original sentence

EXAMPLE: *An encyclopedia is a good source of true facts.*

Improved sentence

An encyclopedia is a good source of facts.

(Since facts are true by their nature, the word "true" repeats information and should be taken out of the sentence.)

Read each sentence below and remove the word or words that repeat information. Then write your new sentence on the writing line(s).

1. The company promised to send me a free gift.

_____

2. Our teacher told us to be quiet and stop talking.

_____

3. I told the children to put away the balls, dolls, and toys.

_____

4. The dog was hungry and needed food.

_____

5. The prisoner lost his freedom and liberty.

_____

6. At the fast-food restaurant, I bought a milk shake, some French fries, some cookies, and junk food.

_____

_____

7. The woman gave birth to two twins.

_____

PROOFREADING

Recognizing proofreading marks

If you need help with grammar, capitalization, or punctuation, refer to the Reference Guide on pages 111–123.

Proofreading Marks

Mark	Meaning	Example
⊙ or .	Add a period.	Time flies⊙
?	Add a question mark.	How ?
!	Add an exclamation point.	They fly too fast !
⋀ or ,	Add a comma.	Bozo, however⋀was wrong.
∽	Reverse the order.	Sue a∩d Jim were right.
≡	Capitalize the letter.	she came late.
/	Make this a small letter.	I'm taking History.
⌒	Close up this space.	I'm le⌒arning about dead people.
⋀	Add whatever is missing.	Bob took⋀class in cooking.
⌣ or "	Add quotation marks.	Lisa said, "The food here is great."
⌄ or '	Add an apostrophe.	It's time to fly.
ℯ	Take this out.	I'm not ~~not~~ crazy.
¶	Indent to begin a new paragraph.	¶ Every age has its fads. Girls in the 1950s wore poodle skirts.

The chart above will help you correct these sentences. Write the corrected sentences on the writing lines.

1. "Did you know that the grand Canyon is 277 miles long?"

_____

2. ¶ "Wow! No, I didn't."

_____

3. ¶ "Some parts of it are a mile deep."

_____

4. ¶ "And it's full of ~~of~~ wild Burros."

_____

PROOFREADING

Recognizing proofreading marks

If you need help with grammar, capitalization, or punctuation, refer to the Reference Guide on pages 111–123.

On the lines below, rewrite the paragraph given on the right. Use the proofreading marks in the paragraph to help you correct it.

People have always ~~always~~ been afraid of ghosts—and some times with good reason. In the West Indies, a family put its dead into a cemetery vault. After a funeral, the coffin was put on a shelf and the vault was locked. ~~But~~ the family's cofins never stayed where they were put, however. Each time the family members went to the vault, they found the coffins standing up. so they decided to cemeth the door shut Now no one could get in. Still, the next time the vault was opened, the coffins had moved again. "How could that be you might ask. No one knows— at least no one living.

PROOFREADING

Using proofreading marks

If you need help with grammar, capitalization, or punctuation, refer to the Reference Guide on pages 111–123.

Proofread the copy given on the right. Use the proofreading marks on page 110 to show what corrections need to be made. Then write the corrected copy on the lines below.

Have you ever heard of the Bermuda Triangle Its a place just off the coast florida. In 1945, five planes disappeared there. An other plane was sent to find them but it disapperaed, too. The next day, 300 Planes and 21 Ships looked for the missing planes. They couldnt find aanything—not even plane wrecks. The lost planes were never hear from again. Since then, many more more planes and ships have disappeared in same place Scientists have studied the area. they have heard strange noises but they don't know what the noises mean..They have searched the ocean floor but they have n't found anything. The mystery remains

_____

_____

_____

_____

_____

_____

_____

_____

_____

PARAGRAPHS

Keeping to the topic

If you need help with grammar, capitalization, or punctuation, refer to the Reference Guide on pages 111–123.

In clear writing, all the sentences in a paragraph focus on the topic, or subject, of the paragraph. Each paragraph given here contains one sentence that moves away from the paragraph's topic. Find the sentence and write it on the lines that follow the paragraph.

A town in England weighs its political leaders every year. It has done this for hundreds of years. The idea is to see if the leaders are getting fat at the public's expense. Of course, a lot of people have weight problems. The town uses a fancy scale with a plush red seat. The officials are weighed in public, and many townspeople attend the ceremony.

_____

_____

On May 25, 1912, Lafayette College and the Carlisle Indian School came together for a track meet. Lafayette College was unbeaten. It also had 48 men on its team, while Carlisle Indian School had only six on its team. One of the six was Jim Thorpe. Thorpe was later stripped of his Olympic track medals because he had played professional baseball. At the track meet, Thorpe won the high jump, broad jump, shot put, discus, 120-yard high hurdles, and 220-yard low hurdles. As a result, Carlisle won the meet, 71–41.

_____

_____

Richard Rodgers and Oscar Hammerstein worked together to write a number of very famous musicals. Hammerstein also worked with other composers. *Oklahoma!*, a Rodgers and Hammerstein musical, won a Pulitzer prize. The two composers also wrote the shows *Carousel, The King and I, Flower Drum Song, The Sound of Music*, and *South Pacific*.

_____

_____

PARAGRAPHS

Keeping to the topic

If you need help with grammar, capitalization, or punctuation, refer to the Reference Guide on pages 111–123.

The *topic sentence* expresses the main idea of a paragraph. It usually goes at either the beginning or the end of the paragraph. Find the topic sentence in each paragraph given here, and write the sentence on the lines that follow the paragraph.

Only once has a midget played professional baseball. On August 19, 1951, Eddie Gaedel went to bat for the St. Louis Browns. He was only 3 feet, 7 inches tall. The number on his shirt was ⅛. The pitcher was laughing so hard that he could hardly pitch. But because Gaedel's strike zone was only 1½ feet long, any pitcher would have had a hard time pitching to him. He was walked and replaced at first base by a pinch runner. Despite Gaedel's help, the Browns lost.

_____

_____

Austria's ruler didn't like to have any wrinkles on his clothes, so he had himself sewn into them. That way there were no buttons or zippers to form bumps or wrinkles. On June 28, 1914, the archduke was shot. Those trying to help him had trouble taking his clothes off. By the time they found scissors, he had bled to death. Archduke Ferdinand's vanity had cost him his life.

_____

_____

One shopping mall in Edmonton, Canada, is almost like an amusement park. For a few dollars, visitors can take a submarine ride. The submarine goes to the bottom of a lake that is 32 feet deep. From the submarine, people can watch mechanical sharks and skin divers swim by. The mall also has a miniature golf course, a zoo, an aquarium, and 24 amusement rides. If you still get bored, you can always go shopping.

_____

_____

PARAGRAPHS

Organizing paragraphs

If you need help with grammar, capitalization, or punctuation, refer to the Reference Guide on pages 111–123.

The following sentences all belong in the same paragraph, but they are out of order. Decide what order they belong in, and then write the sentences in a paragraph on the writing lines.

1. As the gang members left the train, they asked the conductor to send the notice to the newspapers.
2. Soon after they boarded the train, one gang member gave the conductor a written notice.
3. Thus, the James gang did what few robbers do—they wrote their own press release.
4. On January 31, 1874, Jesse James and his gang robbed a train.
5. Actually, there had been ten robbers.
6. The notice described the train robbery.
7. The description said that five men had robbed the train.
8. The notice also said the robbers had headed south, though they really headed west.

PARAGRAPHS
Organizing paragraphs

If you need help with grammar, capitalization, or punctuation, refer to the Reference Guide on pages 111–123.

Before you write a paragraph, it sometimes helps to ask questions about your topic. The answers often give you ideas for the paragraph. Read the questions and answers given on the right. On the line before each question, write the order in which you want to use the information. Write a "1" before the item you want to use first, a "2" before the item you want to use second, and so on.

_____ Topic? St. Valentine's Day Massacre

_____ Who was involved? Al Capone and his men on one side, and the "Bugs" Moran gang on the other

_____ Who were these people? Gangsters

_____ Why was it a massacre? Capone and his men tricked the members of the Moran gang. Then they killed them while they were helpless.

_____ What happened? While pretending to be police officers, Capone and his men "arrested" seven members of Moran's gang. They lined them up against a wall and shot them.

_____ Why were the gangs enemies? They were fighting for control of illegal operations in Chicago.

_____ When did the massacre happen? February 14, 1929 (St. Valentine's Day)

Now write a topic sentence for a paragraph on the St. Valentine's Day Massacre.

_____

_____

Now write a paragraph on the St. Valentine's Day Massacre.

_____

_____

_____

_____

_____

_____

_____

PARAGRAPHS

Organizing paragraphs

If you need help with grammar, capitalization, or punctuation, refer to the Reference Guide on pages 111–123.

Make up answers to the following questions. Then organize your material and use it to write a paragraph on the lines at the bottom of the page. Don't forget to include the topic sentence.

Topic sentence: My friend Tom has the best job imaginable.

What is Tom's job? _____

Where is it? _____

When does he work? _____

How much does the job pay? _____

Whom does Tom work for? _____

Whom does he work with? _____

What does Tom do? _____

_____

Why is Tom's job better than other jobs? _____

_____

Paragraph

_____

_____

_____

_____

_____

_____

_____

_____

_____

PARAGRAPHS

Organizing paragraphs

If you need help with grammar, capitalization, or punctuation, refer to the Reference Guide on pages 111–123.

Make up answers to the following questions. Then organize your material and use it to write a paragraph on the lines at the bottom of the page. Include the topic sentence.

Topic sentence: My boss can sometimes be very unreasonable.

Who is my boss? _____

Where is my job? _____

What is my job? _____

What are my job duties? _____
_____

What does my boss do that is unreasonable? _____
_____

How do I respond? _____
_____

How often is my boss unreasonable? _____

What causes my boss to be unreasonable? _____
_____

What is my boss's general personality? _____
_____

Paragraph

_____

_____

_____

_____

_____

_____

PARAGRAPHS

Organizing paragraphs

If you need help with grammar, capitalization, or punctuation, refer to the Reference Guide on pages 111–123.

Choose and complete one of the following topic sentences, or write one of your own. Ask yourself some questions about your topic, answer those questions, and then organize your material. On the lines at the bottom of the page, write a paragraph on the topic.

1. Ten years from now, I hope to _____

   _____

2. I wish I had acted differently when _____

   _____

3. (Your own topic) _____

   _____

Questions and answers

_____

_____

_____

_____

_____

Paragraph

_____

_____

_____

_____

_____

_____

_____

PARAGRAPHS

Avoiding repetition

If you need help with grammar, capitalization, or punctuation, refer to the Reference Guide on pages 111–123.

The paragraph given on the right is repetitious. Read it carefully and cross out any words or sentences that repeat information. Then write what is left on the lines below.

In the modern times of our day and age, our society today is always changing. Things didn't change as fast when our mothers and fathers were young. Their world moved more slowly. Things didn't move as fast then as they do now. Just think about all the things we have that our parents didn't have. Because our parents didn't have them, they didn't have as many worries. For us, things sometimes seem to change day to day from one day to the next. Just as soon as we get used to something and adjust to it, it changes. Tomorrow's never the same as today. It's a true fact that our society today is certainly fast paced.

_____

_____

_____

_____

_____

_____

_____

_____

You probably discovered that the original paragraph used a lot of words to say very little. But the paragraph did contain an important idea. Ask yourself some questions about the sentences you wrote, and write the questions on the lines at the top of the next page. Then answer the questions, and write your answers next to the questions. Your answers should help you write a better paragraph. Write your new paragraph on the lines at the bottom of the next page.

Questions and answers

New paragraph

PARAGRAPHS

Time-order paragraphs

If you need help with grammar, capitalization, or punctuation, refer to the Reference Guide on pages 111–123.

The following sentences are out of time order. Read them and decide what the best order for the sentences would be if they were used to form a paragraph.

1. He couldn't remember why he had set the alarm to go off so early.
2. Steve jumped out of bed, dressed, and put his gear in his truck.
3. Steve struggled to wake up.
4. Steve's alarm clock shrieked.
5. He raced over to Todd's house.
6. It was still dark outside.
7. He remembered he was supposed to meet Todd to go fishing.

In what numerical order would you put the sentences?

Read the sentences below and decide what the best time order for them would be if they were used to form a paragraph.

1. Todd said to Steve, "Hey, this basket really stinks! Is this your bait?"
2. They drove 50 miles to their secret fishing hole.
3. "No," Steve said. "That's our lunch."
4. Todd finished breakfast.
5. They unloaded the truck.
6. Steve waited.
7. They loaded Todd's gear into the truck.

In what numerical order would you put the sentences?

PARAGRAPHS

Time-order paragraphs

If you need help with grammar, capitalization, or punctuation, refer to the Reference Guide on pages 111–123.

Now write two paragraphs using the sentences given on page 34. The first paragraph should contain the first group of sentences from page 34. The other paragraph should contain the second group of sentences from page 34. Be sure to write the sentences in the new time order you have chosen. In your paragraphs, use time-order words from the list below to show how the events are connected. Then write a third paragraph that tells what happened on the fishing trip. Be sure to use time-order words in that paragraph, too.

after	while	soon	that afternoon
before	when	whenever	the next day
next	later	then	in an hour

_____

_____

_____

_____

_____

_____

_____

_____

_____

_____

_____

_____

_____

_____

_____

PARAGRAPHS

Descriptive paragraphs

If you need help with grammar, capitalization, or punctuation, refer to the Reference Guide on pages 111–123.

Think about a person you feel strongly about. The person can be real or fictional. Then take notes below. Use as many descriptive words as you can think of for each item.

Hair: _____

Eyes: _____

Nose: _____

Ears: _____

Mouth: _____

Skin: _____

Height, weight, and shape: _____

_____

Usual clothing: _____

_____

What he or she likes to do: _____

_____

_____

What he or she doesn't like to do: _____

_____

_____

How he or she acts around other people: _____

_____

_____

What kind of mood he or she is usually in: _____

_____

_____

PARAGRAPHS

Descriptive paragraphs

If you need help with grammar, capitalization, or punctuation, refer to the Reference Guide on pages 111–123.

Use the notes you made on page 36 to write two descriptive paragraphs on the lines below. In your first paragraph, describe the person's physical appearance. In the second paragraph, describe what the person is like.

_____

_____

_____

_____

_____

_____

_____

_____

_____

_____

_____

_____

_____

_____

_____

_____

_____

_____

_____

_____

_____

_____

_____

_____

PARAGRAPHS

Descriptive paragraphs

If you need help with grammar, capitalization, or punctuation, refer to the Reference Guide on pages 111–123.

Four topics for descriptive paragraphs are given on the right. Choose one that interests you, or make up your own topic. Make notes on the topic on the first set of lines below, and then write a descriptive paragraph at the bottom of the page.

1. A rock concert or music video
2. My favorite current fashion
3. My favorite eating place
4. The place where I grew up
5. (Your own topic) _____

_____

Notes

_____

_____

_____

_____

_____

Paragraph

_____

_____

_____

_____

_____

_____

_____

_____

PARAGRAPHS

Factual paragraphs

If you need help with grammar, capitalization, or punctuation, refer to the Reference Guide on pages 111–123.

Read the following notes for a factual paragraph. Organize the notes and then use them to write a paragraph on the writing lines.

1. Robinson Crusoe not a real man, but based on a real man—Alexander Selkirk.

2. Soon Selkirk ran down goats, using them for food and clothing.

3. Spent first night in a tree, scared.

4. Back in England, couldn't get used to civilization. Built cave in backyard. Taught alley cats to dance.

5. Selkirk asked to be put ashore on desert island because ship he was on leaked.

6. For company, made pets of island's cats, teaching them to dance.

7. Gradually got used to living alone on island.

8. Rescued after 4 years and 4 months.

9. At first, stayed next to shore looking for boats, so ate only turtles and fish.

10. After a while, set up home in cave.

_____

_____

_____

_____

_____

_____

_____

_____

_____

_____

_____

PARAGRAPHS

Factual paragraphs

If you need help with grammar, capitalization, or punctuation, refer to the Reference Guide on pages 111–123.

Read the following notes for two paragraphs about the first landing on the moon. Organize the notes and then write the paragraphs on page 41.

First paragraph

Traveled 24,300 mph

On landing, Armstrong's heart rate 156 beats per minute (usually about 75 beats per minute)

Lunar module <u>Eagle</u> carried Armstrong and Aldrin to moon's surface

Three astronauts: Michael Collins, Neil Armstrong, Edwin Aldrin

Traveled 244,930 miles

Apollo 11 took off 9:32 A.M. on July 16, 1969

Landed on moon at 4:17 P.M. on July 20, 1969

Collins stayed in command module and orbited moon

Touchdown location: Sea of Tranquility

Second paragraph

Astronauts supposed to rest for eight hours, but too excited to rest

Astronauts easily hopped high because moon has less gravity than Earth

Opened spaceship door 6½ hours after landing

Brought back to Earth some moon rocks and soil

TV camera turned on so world could watch

Before leaving spaceship, astronauts took three hours to put on space equipment

Armstrong got out first

On airless moon, their footprints probably still remain

Armstrong said moon surface powdery

Left behind on moon cameras, backpacks, tools

Aldrin described view as "magnificent desolation"

PARAGRAPHS

Persuasive paragraphs

If you need help with grammar, capitalization, or punctuation, refer to the Reference Guide on pages 111–123.

Read the question given on the right. Then read the two possible answers below, along with the notes supporting each side. Choose one side to support, and use the notes to write a paragraph supporting your chosen side. You may use your own arguments if you wish. Write your paragraph on the lines at the bottom of the page.

Should the school board create specialty high schools (for example, one for performing arts, one for vocational arts, one for the college-bound)?

Yes, it should

Students should develop their talents

Students would be more interested in school—fewer dropouts

Students are old enough to make own decisions

Would help students get jobs

No, it shouldn't

Everyone should get a general education and specialize later

Too expensive

Transportation problems for students

Students might change their minds

_____

_____

_____

_____

_____

_____

_____

_____

_____

_____

_____

PARAGRAPHS

Persuasive paragraphs

If you need help with grammar, capitalization, or punctuation, refer to the Reference Guide on pages 111–123.

Read the question given on the right. Then read the two possible answers below, along with the notes supporting each side. On the lines below each set of notes, add at least two more arguments to support that side.

Should the number and locations of fast-food restaurants be limited?

Yes, they should be

Bring too many people and
   cars into area
Create litter

No, they shouldn't be

People should have the right
   to set up any business in
   business sections of town
Most other restaurants can't
   provide fast service to
   people in a hurry

_____
_____
_____
_____

_____
_____
_____
_____

Use the notes under the "yes" answer to write a paragraph supporting that side.

_____
_____
_____
_____
_____
_____
_____
_____
_____

Now use the notes under the "no" answer to write a
paragraph supporting that side.

_____

_____

_____

_____

_____

_____

_____

_____

Your two paragraphs are probably one-sided. One-sided
arguments aren't really persuasive. To persuade more people
to share your viewpoint, you need to answer arguments from
the other side. Choose a side, and write a more persuasive
paragraph supporting your choice. Be sure to answer some
arguments from the other side.

_____

_____

_____

_____

_____

_____

_____

_____

_____

_____

_____

PARAGRAPHS

Summary paragraphs

If you need help with grammar, capitalization, or punctuation, refer to the Reference Guide on pages 111–123.

Read the short biography given on the right.

John Merrick is better known as the Elephant Man. He lived in the nineteenth century. He had a disease that made him look almost like an elephant. His skin was rough and thick. A huge growth hung over one eye, and another growth hung from the back of his head. His head was as big as his waist. Bony growths in his mouth made it hard for anyone to understand what he was saying. From his chest and back grew huge bags of flesh.

For a long time, the Elephant Man was a freak in the circus, where he was badly treated. Eventually, he was taken to a hospital. The doctors were not able to cure him, but they did make him comfortable. Merrick lived at the hospital for the rest of his life. As people came to know him, they found that he was intelligent and gentle. Important people came to see him and talk with him. He made many friends, including the queen of England. He said he was very happy, but he was never able to smile. Because of his growths, his face could show no expression.

John Merrick lived only 26 years. He was never able to sleep lying down, because his head was too heavy. But he always wanted to sleep the way other people do. One day he did. His heavy head broke his neck, and John Merrick died.

On the lines below, jot down some notes on the biography. Include only the most important and interesting information.

_____

_____

_____

_____

_____

_____

_____

PARAGRAPHS

Summary paragraphs

If you need help with grammar, capitalization, or punctuation, refer to the Reference Guide on pages 111–123.

Look at the notes you made on page 45. If you could write only one sentence to summarize all of the information, what would it be?

_____

_____

Use the sentence you wrote above as the topic sentence for a paragraph summarizing John Merrick's biography. Write your summary paragraph on the lines below.

_____

_____

_____

_____

_____

_____

_____

_____

_____

_____

_____

_____

_____

_____

FACT/OPINION

Knowing the difference

If you need help with grammar, capitalization, or punctuation, refer to the Reference Guide on pages 111–123.

Most writers use both facts and opinions. It is important to recognize the difference between them. A *fact* is a statement that has been proven; no one can disagree with it. An *opinion* expresses someone's belief; other people may disagree with it.

Fact

EXAMPLE: *Benjamin Franklin wanted to make the turkey our national symbol.*

Opinion

George Washington was a better president than Calvin Coolidge.

Read each sentence below. If it states a fact, write "fact" on the line next to the sentence. If it states an opinion, write "opinion" on the line.

1. Thanksgiving Day is a national holiday. _____

2. In 1900, one-third of the cars in New York, Boston, and Chicago were

   electric. _____

3. Blue is a more becoming color than orange. _____

4. Summer is the best time of year. _____

5. We have never had a president who was an only child. _____

6. Today's fashions are weird. _____

7. There is a city called Peculiar in Missouri. _____

8. My father is better looking than his father. _____

9. Dogs make better pets than cats. _____

10. A woman ran for president of the United States in 1872. _____

11. Democracy is the best form of government. _____

12. Among lions, females do about 90 percent of the hunting. _____

13. City life is more exciting than country life. _____

14. In World War II, the Navajo language was used as a U.S. military code. _____

TRANSITIONS

Showing logical connections

If you need help with grammar, capitalization, or punctuation, refer to the Reference Guide on pages 111–123.

Transition words are words that help show the logical connection between two sentences or paragraphs. The following are common transition words or phrases:

thus	for instance	yet	finally
in addition	of course	in fact	in other words
as a result	therefore	for example	in conclusion
however	in contrast	also	on the other hand
too	similarly	in comparison	

EXAMPLE: *The bones of a 160-pound man weigh 29 pounds.* **In contrast,** *if his bones were made of steel, they would weigh four to five times as much.*

Each pair of sentences below is missing some transition words. For each one, choose a transition word or phrase from the list to help show the connection between the pair of sentences. Write the word or phrase on the line next to the sentence. Don't use any one word or phrase more than once. Remember that transition words are usually followed by commas.

1. The moon has craters. Mars does, _____ .

2. Many people have odd superstitions. _____ one man put dishes of salt under the legs of his bed to get rid of evil spirits.

3. At first, Americans didn't know what to do with tea. _____ they served the tea leaves and threw the tea away.

4. There are four times as many people in the world now as there were 300 years ago. _____ there are a million times as many scientists.

5. In 1985, a volcanic eruption in Colombia caused a huge mudslide. _____ many thousands of people were killed.

6. A man rode over Niagara Falls in a barrel and lived. _____ he later slipped on a banana peel and died.

TRANSITIONS

Showing logical connections

If you need help with grammar, capitalization, or punctuation, refer to the Reference Guide on pages 111–123.

The paragraph given on the right has no transition words between sentences. Add transition words or phrases to the beginnings of at least four sentences. Write your new paragraph on the lines below.

Joseph Miller was an actor in the eighteenth century. Miller wasn't a very good actor. He was a good comic. No matter what the situation, he always had a joke. Sometimes he got credit for other people's jokes. When Joe Miller died, his friends were all he left to his family. He didn't leave them any money. His friends decided to raise money for the family by collecting Joe's jokes. They published a book containing 247 jokes. Many modern jokes are based on Joe Miller's 247 jokes.

Checkpoint 1

If you need help with grammar, capitalization, or punctuation, refer to the Reference Guide on pages 111–123.

The notice given on the right contains many errors. Use the proofreading marks on page 110 to show where corrections need to be made. Then write the corrected notice on the lines at the bottom of the page.

NOTISE   HElp Wanted

Job:	Selling popcorn and candy movie refreshment counter
Salary:	$5.00–$7.50, depending on experience
Location:	United movies 786 Starr St
Dtuies:	Make fresh popcorn before each show. Order candy stock shelves and fill soft drink machines. Wait on customers
Qulifications:	Must be at least at least 16 years old. Must be able to make ch ange accurately. Must have pleasant personality

If interested, contact the manager at United Movies.

_____

_____

_____

_____

_____

_____

_____

_____

_____

_____

You applied for and got the advertised job at United Movies. In three paragraphs, describe your first impression of the place, your co-workers, and your customers. Be sure to make your descriptions lively by using descriptive words. Proofread your paragraphs.

You've been working behind the refreshment counter for three months. Your boss wants to hire someone to help you and has asked you to find someone for the job. You would like to ask your best friend to apply. But your friend has heard you complain about your job and isn't sure about taking one like it. On the lines below, list the things you like and the things you don't like about the job.

Things I like   **Things I don't like**

_____   _____
_____   _____
_____   _____
_____   _____
_____   _____

Now write a paragraph in which you try to persuade your friend to take the job. Remember, your friend has heard your complaints. You have to overcome your friend's objections.

_____
_____
_____
_____
_____
_____
_____
_____
_____
_____
_____
_____

LETTERS

Friendly letters

If you need help with grammar, capitalization, or punctuation, refer to the Reference Guide on pages 111–123.

Read Chris's friendly letter to Terry. Then pretend you are Terry and write a response.

August 25, 1988

Dear Terry,

Aren't you supposed to relax during vacations? I feel as if I've spent the last two weeks in a clothes dryer—spinning around very fast and getting all hot and wrinkled. I visited 21 countries in 14 days. Unfortunately, my suitcases visited 33 countries, but never the same one I was in at the time. It's hard to make new friends when you've been wearing the same socks for two weeks!

But enough about my vacation. How was your trip to the mining camp? Write soon, with lots of juicy details.

Your friend,
Chris

LETTERS

Friendly letters

If you need help with grammar, capitalization, or punctuation, refer to the Reference Guide on pages 111–123.

While you were cleaning out your closet, you discovered a $10,000 bill in an old sock. When she heard about your lucky find, Aunt Kate told you to spend the money on fun. Write a letter telling her how you might do that.

_____

_____

_____

_____

_____

When he heard about your good fortune, Uncle Albert, a stuffy banker, told you to spend the money wisely. Write a letter telling him how you might do that.

_____

_____

_____

_____

_____

LETTERS

Business letters

If you need help with grammar, capitalization, or punctuation, refer to the Reference Guide on pages 111–123.

You have lived in the same apartment for five years. Lately, more and more things have been going wrong with it. You've noticed the following problems (add some of your own on the writing lines):

cockroaches in the kitchen
leaky windows
peeling paint

_____

With your rent check, include a letter of complaint to your landlord. Write the letter on the writing lines below.

261 Crumbling Drive, Apt. 3
Mudville, CA 94072
January 15, 1989

Mr. Thornton Lodge
One Thousand Park Plaza Drive
Lodge City, CA 94073

Dear Mr. Lodge:

_____

_____

_____

_____

_____

_____

_____

_____

_____

(Signature)

_____

(Print your name)

LETTERS

Business letters

If you need help with grammar, capitalization, or punctuation, refer to the Reference Guide on pages 111–123.

Read the advertisement shown below. Then order two books by filling out the order blank at the bottom of the form.

SPECIAL OFFER!

For a limited time only, Chance of a Lifetime, Inc., is able to offer the books listed below at special prices. These books offer you the chance to have the glamorous life you've always wanted. Order your copies today! The books are not available in stores. (All prices include shipping and handling charges.)

Order Number	Title	Price
TY543	*Turn Your Paint-by-Number Hobby into a Million-Dollar Business*	$17.95
HU763	*A Hundred Uses for Corn on the Cob*	$ 6.95
TS891	*Touring the Swiss Alps by Bicycle*	$ 8.95
HB481	*How to Build Your Own Ocean Liner with Things You Have around the House*	$ 7.95

Order Form
Chance of a Lifetime, Inc.

Name _____

Address _____

City/State _____ ZIP _____

Order Number	Quantity	Title	Copy Price	Total Price

Send order blank with check or money order to:
Chance of a Lifetime, Inc., P.O. Box 1954, Chicago, IL 60690

LETTERS

Business letters

If you need help with grammar, capitalization, or punctuation, refer to the Reference Guide on pages 111–123.

After you have mailed the order blank given on page 56, you decide that you would like to order the remaining two books. However, you don't have another order blank. Write a letter to the company that includes all of the information asked for on the order blank.

_____

_____

_____

_____

_____

_____

Dear Chance of a Lifetime, Inc.:

_____

_____

_____

_____

_____

_____

_____

_____

_____

_____

(Signature)

_____

(Print your name)

LETTERS

Employment letters

If you need help with grammar, capitalization, or punctuation, refer to the Reference Guide on pages 111–123.

Use the letter given on the right to help you write your own letter asking about a job. You may ask about a job as a grocery-store checker, gas-station attendant, general office assistant, nurse's aide, or any other type of job that interests you. Write your letter on the lines below. Include a salutation and a complimentary close.

1622 University Avenue
Davis, CA 95616
April 7, 1987

Richard S. Garcia, D.V.M.
91 Walnut Street
Davis, CA 95616

Dear Dr. Garcia:

Do you have an opening for a veterinary assistant? If you do, I would like to apply for the position.

I will be graduating from high school in June, and I will then be available for full-time work. I grew up on a farm and have had experience raising and caring for farm animals and pets. Because I love animals, I would like to learn more about caring for them.

May I call you to arrange for an interview?

Sincerely,

Carl Thomas

Carl Thomas

LETTERS

Employment letters

If you need help with grammar, capitalization, or punctuation, refer to the Reference Guide on pages 111–123.

Read the following want ads. Then write a letter expressing interest in one of the jobs. Be sure to give a brief explanation of your qualifications. You may make up information if you wish. Write your letter on the lines at the bottom of the page.

**SALESPERSON
RECORD STORE**

Must be knowledgeable about all kinds of music. Good at handling money. Good with people. No experience necessary. Write to: Mr. William Benson, P.O. Box 983, Los Angeles, CA 90053.

PLAYGROUND DIRECTOR

Must be very good with children of all ages. Good at organizing games, sports. Job involves keeping track of equipment. Athletic ability preferred. No experience needed. Contact: Ms. Sharon Ong, Parkview Playground, 615 Monroe Ave., Baltimore, MD 21224

LETTERS

Employment letters

If you need help with grammar, capitalization, or punctuation, refer to the Reference Guide on pages 111–123.

You were recently interviewed for a job as a mail-room clerk at Kelley Office Machines, Inc. You want to write a thank-you letter to Mr. O'Rourke, who interviewed you. At the time of the interview, you told Mr. O'Rourke that you could start work on October 13. Mr. O'Rourke, however, said that he hopes to hire someone who can start at the beginning of the month. Since the interview, you have learned that you could start the job on October 2. You want to let Mr. O'Rourke know that. Finish the thank-you letter begun on the lines below.

_____

_____

_____

Mr. Kenneth O'Rourke
Kelley Office Machines, Inc.
444 Market Street
Linden, VA 22642

_____

_____

_____

_____

_____

_____

_____

_____

_____

_____

_____

RÉSUMÉS

Summaries of job qualifications

If you need help with grammar, capitalization, or punctuation, refer to the Reference Guide on pages 111–123.

A *résumé* is a short account of a person's education, experience, and skills. It gives an employer the means to assess a job applicant's qualifications.

Use the paragraph and model résumé below to write a résumé for your imaginary friend Clayton Lee. Make up any extra information you need, and write the résumé on the lines given on page 62.

Your friend Clayton Lee is looking for a job. He has asked you to help him prepare his résumé. Clayton is working this summer as a fry cook at a fast-food restaurant. He will graduate next June from Benjamin Franklin High School. During the past school year, Clayton worked part-time stocking shelves in an auto-parts store. In school, he has taken several classes in programming. He has also coached the local Little League team for the past two years.

```
                          JANET C. BRENNAN
                          1735 Alpine Way
                       Denver, Colorado 80228
                          (303) 569-2247

EDUCATION            Rocky Mountain High School
                     Denver, Colorado

                       Graduated June 1986
                       Courses of interest:

                         Biology I, II      Earth Science
                         Botany             Applied Math


WORK EXPERIENCE

6/85 - 5/86          Gardener's Helper, Rios Gardening, 887 Fairview
                     Avenue, Denver, CO 80220.  Assisted firm owner
                     with groundskeeping and planting of gardens.
                     Made frequent trips to the nursery.  Helped to
                     plan and execute two custom landscaping projects.

11/84 - 12/84        Gift Wrapper, Harmon's Department Store, Midtown
                     Mall, Oak and Third Streets, Denver, CO 80204.
                     Wrapped gifts for customers during Christmas
                     rush.  Occasionally operated cash register and
                     handled money.  Learned inventory procedures
                     during post-holiday inventory.

Summer 1984          Office Clerk, Brennan Associates, 2768 Parker
                     Boulevard, Denver, CO 80226.  Performed general
                     office duties including typing, filing, envelope
                     stuffing, and running errands.


COMMUNITY ACTIVITIES

8/85 - Present       Serve as a volunteer at the Children's Science
                     Center.  Lead local nature walks for children.


SKILLS               Speak and write Spanish fluently.
                     Type 45 wpm.
                     Have excellent sewing skills.


REFERENCES           Available upon request.
```

_____

_____

_____

_____

EDUCATION
_____

_____

_____

_____

_____   _____

_____   _____

WORK EXPERIENCE

_____   _____

                                          _____

                                          _____

                                          _____

                                          _____

_____   _____

                                          _____

                                          _____

COMMUNITY ACTIVITIES

_____   _____

                                          _____

SKILLS   _____

                                          _____

                                          _____

REFERENCES   _____

RÉSUMÉS

Summaries of job qualifications

If you need help with grammar, capitalization, or punctuation, refer to the Reference Guide on pages 111–123.

Now write a résumé for yourself. If you need help, look back at the model résumé on page 61 and the résumé you wrote for Clayton Lee on page 62.

Checkpoint 2

Fill out the job application form given below. You may make up information if you wish.

Job Application

Position: Camp Counselor

_____
Date

Name: _____
        First Name   Initial   Last Name

Address: _____
        Number and Street   Apt. No.

_____
        City   State   ZIP

Birthdate: _____
        Month   Date   Year

Put a check next to the camp sessions for which you are available.

_____ June 15–July 6   _____ July 10–July 31   _____ August 4–August 25

Briefly describe your previous jobs (paid and volunteer). Indicate the dates you held the jobs.

_____

_____

_____

_____

_____

Write two or three sentences explaining why you think you would be good at this job.

_____

_____

_____

Ms. Larsen has sent you a letter offering you a job as a camp counselor. In the letter, she asked you what camp activities you would like to plan and what supplies you will need. Write a reply on the lines below. Make sure you say that you are accepting the job.

_____
_____
_____

Ms. Judy Larsen, Director
Camp Three Rivers
Ducks' Landing
White Falls, OR 97601

_____

_____
_____
_____
_____
_____
_____
_____
_____
_____
_____
_____
_____

_____
_____
_____

Part of your job as a camp counselor is to help the children write their letters home. Here are some of their letters. Use the proofreading marks on page 110 to correct the letters. Watch out for *homophones*. Homophones are words that sound the same but have different spellings and meanings. For example, "some" and "sum" are homophones.

august 12, 1988

Deer mom and DaD,

To day was realy eggsiting. We went on a Hike. I gott lost for a littel while. I wasnt scared at all, not even wen a lion ate my backpack! Plese send me a knew backpack.

Love, Pete

August 12, 1988

Dear grand ma

Thank you for the kookies. Jenny and i eight them in our tnet last night. Jenny was to sick for brake fast this morning. So i got to ate her pancakes Tonite were going too roast marshmallows. Camp is so much fun!

Love, Brenda

Agust 12, 1988

dear Mom,

Are tent has has a new pet. We found it last night under a roc. It's name is Mr Slithers. To night it get to slepe with me! gcss what mr. Slithers is. Can i kepe him

Your dauhter, Sally

Augus 12, 1988

Dear Dad,

    I have a little problem. Don't get mad, OK? Today a
beer was chasing my friend Pete. I through my backpack
at the bare. He ate it! So now I need a new backpack. This
time, could you Get blew. Beers dont like blew.

                Love, Tim

August 12, 1988

Dear Mom and Dad,

Do think i culd cum home erly. I dint mind the poison oke
or the mosquito bits. I dint even mind all most drowning
or falling down that clif. but now things are terribel! Plese
cum get me <u>fast!</u>

                Your sun, Alan

August 12, 1988

Dear ant judy,

    Camp is relly tiring. Were up with the chikins—at six
o'cluck! Then we have to make breakfast for all the kamp
kounselors. Then we have to swepe out there tents. After
our hike we make lunch. Then we wash the dishs while
we go swiming. I shuld have stayd home!

                Love, Patty

On the lines below, write a friendly letter to a friend or
relative telling about your experiences as a camp counselor.
Use some of the experiences described in the children's
letters, or make up your own. Write at least two paragraphs.

REPORTS

Report of an interview

If you need help with grammar, capitalization, or punctuation, refer to the Reference Guide on pages 111–123.

You have been asked to interview someone who grew up in another country. You decide to interview your neighbor, Angelina Rossi. Use your questions and her answers below to help you write a report about her. Give your report a title, and write it on the lines at the bottom of the page.

When were you born? In 1911.

Where were you born? In Marineo, a small village near Palermo, Italy.

What did your father do? He owned a small grove of olive trees. Many of the people in the village were small farmers like us. Others were fishermen.

What do you remember most about your house in Italy? My favorite room was the kitchen. It was always cheerful and full of good smells.

What kind of food did you eat? Well, like many Italians, we often ate pasta. We always used a lot of tomato sauce and garlic—and naturally, lots of olive oil.

Why did you and your family come to this country? We came in 1925 because my father thought life would be better here. My father opened a little grocery store in North Beach in San Francisco. There were many other Italians living there, so we soon felt right at home.

REPORTS

Book reports

If you need help with grammar, capitalization, or punctuation, refer to the Reference Guide on pages 111–123.

Read the sample book report on the left below. Then read the notes on the right, describing the book Death in the Orchard by Apricot R. Burr.

```
                      BOOK REPORT

Title:  Spies in the Garden

Author:  Daisy Waters

Setting:  Pleasanton, a quiet suburb of Washington, D.C.

Main Characters:  Lily Flowers, William Flowers, Petals,
                  and Melanie Weed

Plot:  Lily and William Flowers live with their two children

       and their dog Petals in Pleasanton.  One day, Petals

       is digging in the backyard.  He finds a roll of

       microfilm and brings it inside.  When a secret agent

       comes to the house for the microfilm, Lily Flowers

       becomes a member of his spy ring.  She and Petals

       have many exciting adventures.  They capture the

       famous double agent, Melanie Weed.  Lily's biggest

       problem is getting home in time to fix dinner for

       her family.  Her husband and children don't know

       she is a spy.

Recommendation:

This book is often very funny because most of the people in it

don't know Lily Flowers is a spy.  I recommend the book to anyone

who likes funny, exciting stories.
```

Notes on Death in the Orchard by Apricot R. Burr

About murder of A. J. Applegate. His body found in orchard on his estate. Estate is called Applegate Manor. Body found by dog. Dog's name is Peaches. Detective called in to solve murder—Sam Fawcett.

Suspects:

Granddaughter, Cherry Applegate. Her grandfather cut her out of his will.

Nephew, Barry Vine. Had stolen $150,000 from Applegate Industries.

Driver, Arthur Spruce. Applegate had driven Spruce's wife crazy. She's in a mental institution.

Secretary, Stella Scribe. Applegate had bullied her for years.

Sam Fawcett solves murder.

Now use the notes on Death in the Orchard to write a book report. Use the model above for the form of your report. Write your report on the lines given on page 71.

REPORTS
Weather reports

If you need help with grammar, capitalization, or punctuation, refer to the Reference Guide on pages 111–123.

On the lines below, take notes about today's weather. Then use your notes to write a weather report.

Approximate outside temperature: _____ Sky: _____

Wind: _____ Precipitation: _____

Forecast for later today and this evening: _____

_____

Weather Report

Date: _____

_____

_____

_____

_____

Eyewitness reports

Look at the picture below. Make detailed notes on a separate sheet of paper about what you see.

Eyewitness reports

If you need help with grammar, capitalization, or punctuation, refer to the Reference Guide on pages 111–123.

Cover the picture on page 72 so you can't see it. Use the notes you took about the picture to help you write an eyewitness report describing the scene. Give your report a title, and write it on the lines below.

_____

_____

_____

_____

_____

_____

_____

_____

_____

_____

_____

_____

_____

_____

_____

_____

_____

_____

_____

REPORTS

Research reports

If you need help with grammar, capitalization, or punctuation, refer to the Reference Guide on pages 111–123.

When preparing to write a research report, it is helpful to first organize your notes in outline form. When you outline, you arrange your notes in the order you will use to present the ideas in your paper. You group related ideas under subject headings and rank the ideas in order of importance. A formal outline includes a title, main ideas, supporting ideas, examples of supporting ideas, and details.

Some notes on Charlie Parkhurst are given on the right. On a separate sheet of paper, write an outline of the information given in the notes. Be sure to include a title and subject headings.

Everyone thought she was a man—5 feet, 7 inches tall; broad shoulders; chewed tobacco; gambled.

Died December 31, 1879.

When grown, disguised herself as a man and became a stagecoach driver.

Born Charlotte Parkhurst.

Once there, got job with California Stage Company.

Grew up in New Hampshire orphanage.

Became a stableboy in Massachusetts.

Once drove across collapsing bridge.

Retired in late 1860s to Watsonville, California.

Ran away from orphanage dressed in boys' clothes.

Once shot highway robbers, saving coach and passengers.

Went to California in 1851 during Gold Rush.

When neighbors were getting body ready for burial, they found that Charlie was a woman.

One of the company's best and bravest drivers.

Called herself "Charlie."

REPORTS

Research reports

If you need help with grammar, capitalization, or punctuation, refer to the Reference Guide on pages 111–123.

Now use your outline to help you write a report about Charlie Parkhurst. Write as many paragraphs as you have main ideas in your outline. Be sure to give your report a title.

CLASSIFICATION

Items within a class

If you need help with grammar, capitalization, or punctuation, refer to the Reference Guide on pages 111–123.

The foods and beverages listed below are served at The Jocks' 'n' Jills' Cafe. Write the items under their proper category headings on the menu at the bottom of the page.

O. J.
Heavy-Hitter Sundae
Touchdown Burger
Cubs' Cupcakes
49er Franks 'n' Beans
Ham 'n' Turkey Double-
 Header Sandwich
Yankee Cherry Pie
Jet Black Coffee

Sea Hawk Fish 'n' Chips
First-Down Chef's Salad
Packers' Pizza
Red-Dog Hot Dog
Sox Soda
Baseball Club Sandwich
Triple-Play Chicken Salad
L. A. Ramsteak Sandwich
Met Milk Shake

The Jocks' 'n' Jills' Cafe

Hot or Cold Sandwiches

_____

_____

_____

_____

_____

Hot Entrées

_____

_____

_____

Salads

_____

_____

Desserts

_____

_____

_____

Beverages

_____

_____

_____

_____

76

CLASSIFICATION

Differences within a class

If you need help with grammar, capitalization, or punctuation, refer to the Reference Guide on pages 111–123.

Four general categories are listed below. Choose one that interests you or make up one of your own. Then, to the right of your chosen category, list four items that belong in that category.

1. High schools in your area

2. Athletes

3. Rock groups

4. Horror movies

5. (Your own category) _____

_____

_____
Category

_____

_____

_____

All the items you listed have something in common. That's why they all belong in the same category. But there are also differences between them. On the lines below, write a paragraph in which you describe the items' *differences*.

_____

_____

_____

_____

_____

_____

_____

_____

_____

_____

_____

IMAGINATION

Figures of speech

If you need help with grammar, capitalization, or punctuation, refer to the Reference Guide on pages 111–123.

Writing can be made more colorful by the use of *figures of speech*. These are words or phrases used imaginatively rather than literally. A *simile* is one kind of figure of speech. It is a comparison of two unlike things, preceded by *like* or *as*.

EXAMPLE: *That hamburger was as tasty as an old shoe.*

A *metaphor* is another kind of figure of speech. It *implies* a comparison of unlike things, omitting *like* or *as*.

EXAMPLE: *Eating chocolate ice cream with marshmallow sauce is sheer heaven.*

Complete the following sentences with similes or metaphors.

1. Larry is as tall as _____.

2. Riding in a space shuttle will be _____.

3. I woke up this morning _____.

4. My brother is as graceful as _____.

5. Diane's room looks like _____.

6. My trip on the ocean liner was _____.

7. Maria sings like a _____.

8. The rain on the roof sounded like _____.

9. Passing a test is _____.

10. Job interviews are _____.

11. When she gets angry, my mother looks like _____.

12. Washing dishes is as exciting as _____.

13. The light hitting the window was _____.

14. Thanksgiving dinner is _____.

15. That movie was _____.

IMAGINATION

Expressions

If you need help with grammar, capitalization, or punctuation, refer to the Reference Guide on pages 111–123.

Some commonly used imaginative expressions are listed below. Choose six of them. Then, on the lines below, tell what each expression means and explain how the picture that comes to mind fits the meaning of the expression.

Fly off the handle
Makes my blood boil
Get a kick out of something
Let the cat out of the bag
Off the top of my head
To be all thumbs

Find a needle in a haystack
It's on the tip of my tongue
The nuts and bolts
Off the wall
Blind as a bat
Dead as a doornail

Give someone a piece of your mind
Go out on a limb
Take the words right out of my mouth
To have a thick (or thin) skin

1. _____

_____

_____

2. _____

_____

_____

3. _____

_____

_____

4. _____

_____

_____

5. _____

_____

_____

6. _____

_____

_____

DESCRIPTIONS

Describing what you see

If you need help with grammar, capitalization, or punctuation, refer to the Reference Guide on pages 111–123.

1.

2.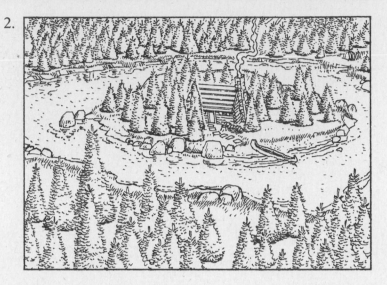

Look at the pictures given above. On the lines below, write a paragraph about each picture, relating the picture to someone or something you know.

1. _____

_____

_____

_____

_____

_____

_____

2. _____

_____

_____

_____

_____

_____

DESCRIPTIONS

Describing what you imagine

If you need help with grammar, capitalization, or punctuation, refer to the Reference Guide on pages 111–123.

Six settings are listed below. Choose two settings that interest you. Then write a description of each on the lines that follow. Don't tell a story; just describe what you see. Make your descriptions as colorful as you can.

an amusement park	a sports event	a bench in a park
a picnic	a city bus	a store's electronics department

1. _____

_____

_____

_____

_____

_____

_____

_____

_____

2. _____

_____

_____

_____

_____

_____

_____

_____

_____

DESCRIPTIONS

Describing what you imagine

If you need help with grammar, capitalization, or punctuation, refer to the Reference Guide on pages 111–123.

Three settings and three items are listed below. Choose one setting from the first column and one item from the second column. Then write a description of each on the lines that follow. Don't tell a story; just describe what you see. Make your descriptions as colorful as you can.

a cemetery   a magazine cover
a haunted house   one piece of clothing
a murder scene   a television set (turned off)

1. _____

_____

_____

_____

_____

_____

_____

_____

2. _____

_____

_____

_____

_____

_____

_____

_____

POEMS

Writing in verse

If you need help with grammar, capitalization, or punctuation, refer to the Reference Guide on pages 111–123.

Read the limerick given on the right.

Said a slithering worm to its mate,
"Have you heard of a worm's final fate?
    First we're made to eat dirt
    Till our poor bellies hurt.
Then we're cut into fishermen's bait."

Now finish the next two limericks, adding rhyming words.

There once was a strange, little man
Who had an impossible _____ .
    He wanted to _____ .
    He gave it a try,
And he landed right in the trash _____ .

There once was a lady named _____
Who invented a washing machine.
    As it started to rock,
    It ate up a _____ .
And nothing came out very _____ .

Now write two of your own limericks on the lines below.

_____

_____

_____

_____

_____

_____

_____

_____

STORIES

Titles for stories

If you need help with grammar, capitalization, or punctuation, refer to the Reference Guide on pages 111–123.

Make up three titles for mystery stories.

_____

_____

_____

Make up three titles for science fiction stories.

_____

_____

_____

Make up three titles for western stories.

_____

_____

_____

Make up three titles for romance stories.

_____

_____

_____

Make up three titles for humorous stories.

_____

_____

_____

STORIES

Dialogue in stories

If you need help with grammar, capitalization, or punctuation, refer to the Reference Guide on pages 111–123.

Read the paragraph given on the right. Then write a dialogue about the situation on the lines below. Base some of your dialogue on the contents of the paragraph, but create some new dialogue ideas as well. Don't forget to use quotation marks.

Elaine and Brad were thinking of moving. Elaine wanted to move to the country. She said that she would enjoy the fresh air and open spaces. She liked the idea of knowing her neighbors. But Brad wanted to stay in the big city. He liked the fast-paced life, the crowds, and the many things to do.

Elaine said, _____

_____

_____

Brad replied, _____

_____

_____

Elaine argued, _____

_____

_____

Brad claimed, _____

_____

_____

Elaine answered, _____

_____

_____

Brad exclaimed, _____

_____

_____

STORIES

Beginnings and endings of stories

If you need help with grammar, capitalization, or punctuation, refer to the Reference Guide on pages 111–123.

The beginning of a story is given on the right. Finish the story on the lines below and give the story a title.

_____
(Title)

One Sunday evening, Mr. and Mrs. North were driving along a lonely country road in southern Idaho. Mrs. North looked off toward the west and said to her husband, "What a beautiful sunset! I don't think I've ever seen such a fiery red glow."

They drove along in silence for the next hour. Then Mr. North said, "I'm surprised it's still so light. The sun certainly is taking a long time to set tonight."

Mrs. North replied, "And the colors are still so bright! Let's stop by the side of the road and just watch for a little while."

"If it's OK with you," Mr. North suggested, "I'd rather get to the top of this hill first. Besides, we'll get a better view from there."

So they drove to the top of the hill. In the valley below, they saw not the sun but a large metallic disc. From it came a fiery red glow and a low whirring hum. As the Norths watched in horror, a lid on the disc began to open.

_____

_____

_____

_____

_____

_____

_____

_____

STORIES

Beginnings and endings of stories

If you need help with grammar, capitalization, or punctuation, refer to the Reference Guide on pages 111–123.

The ending of a story is given below the writing lines. Write a beginning for the story, making sure to describe what the lost object is and how it got lost. Give the story a title.

_____

_____

_____

_____

_____

_____

_____

_____

They ran after the garbage truck, shouting wildly. But the driver didn't hear them. Soon the truck was miles ahead, on its way to the dump.

"Oh, no!" shrieked Sarah. "What should we do now?"

"We don't have any choice," Ben said. "We have to go to the dump."

They got into Ben's car and drove to the dump. The entire way, Sarah moaned, "How will we ever find such a small thing? It's like looking for a needle in a haystack."

It wasn't long before they reached the dump. The manager told them they were free to look around. Ben slipped and fell into a smelly, greasy mess. "This certainly isn't my idea of a great date!" he complained. "If I'd known you like garbage, we could have cleaned out my garage."

All of a sudden, Sarah spotted what she'd been looking for. Wiping off the coffee grounds and potato peelings, she put it safely in her pocket. "Whew!" she sighed with relief. "Now I don't have to keep hiding from Jason!"

STORIES

Beginnings and endings of stories

If you need help with grammar, capitalization, or punctuation, refer to the Reference Guide on pages 111–123.

The middle of a story is given on the bottom of this page, continuing on the top of page 89. On the lines provided, write a beginning and an ending for the story. Give the story a title.

_____

_____

_____

_____

_____

_____

_____

_____

_____

_____

_____

_____

_____

_____

The famous detective Mickey Spill walked into the room. He took in the details at a glance. "I can tell from the bloodstains," he said, "that this man was not actually stabbed." He picked up the ashtray lying on the desk. A half-smoked cigar lay in it. Mickey was puzzled to see that a pipe was still in the murdered man's hand.

The door opened, and Miss Cook, the murdered man's secretary, walked in. She looked as if she had been crying. "Can you tell me what happened this morning?" Mickey asked her.

"Well," she replied, "Mr. Graves had breakfast with his wife, Molly, at 7:30, his usual time. Something must have happened. He left earlier than usual, looking very angry. At 9:00, he had an appointment with Dr. Franklin for his yearly checkup. He came home looking rather upset. I didn't have a chance to ask him what was wrong. His lawyer, Adam Garfield, was already waiting to see him. Mr. Garfield had been waiting for over half an hour. He said it was very important that he see Mr. Graves as soon as possible. After meeting with his lawyer, Mr. Graves was supposed to have lunch with his daughter, Marilyn. I don't know if he was alive to do that."

"Thank you," said Mickey Spill. "You've been a big help. Now I know the people to talk to next."

STORIES

A complete story

If you need help with grammar, capitalization, or punctuation, refer to the Reference Guide on pages 111–123.

Two story ideas are given below. Choose one of them and use it to write a short story. Write your story on the writing lines on this and the next page. Give the story a title.

1. Marsha is on her way to her dentist's office on the fifteenth floor of the Medical Offices Building. The elevator gets stuck between floors. Looking around, Marsha sees the oddest assortment of people she has ever seen. The elevator is stuck for an hour.

2. Richard is eating a hamburger in a restaurant. He looks around and notices a woman about his age at a nearby table. Something about her interests him. As the woman walks by Richard's table on her way out, she drops a piece of paper onto Richard's plate.

Andrew was looking through the want ads to pass the time. An ad in the "Personals" column caught his eye. It read:

I'm trieing too find find Tony prescott. If you have any information about him plese see Me at 739 wayside St at 8:00 PM on teusday Aug 20. Ask for, Big Ed.

Use the proofreading marks on page 110 to correct the want ad.

Since Andrew did know Tony Prescott, he decided to go see Big Ed. On the lines below, first describe Wayside Street and then describe the building at 739 Wayside Street. Use complete sentences.

_____

_____

_____

_____

_____

_____

_____

_____

_____

_____

_____

_____

_____

_____

Now describe the appearance and personality of each of the following characters. Use complete sentences.

Andrew: _____

_____

_____

_____

_____

_____

_____

Tony Prescott: _____

_____

_____

_____

_____

_____

_____

Big Ed: _____

_____

_____

_____

_____

_____

_____

Describe what Andrew saw when Big Ed opened the door. Again, use complete sentences.

_____

_____

_____

_____

_____

_____

How does Andrew know Tony Prescott?

_____

_____

_____

_____

_____

_____

Why does Big Ed want to find Tony?

_____

_____

_____

_____

_____

_____

What did Andrew and Big Ed say to each other?

_____

_____

_____

_____

_____

_____

_____

Use the ideas you have come up with to write a story about
Andrew, Tony, and Big Ed. Use dialogue in the story. Write
your story on the writing lines on this and the next page.
Give the story a title.

_____

_____

_____

_____

_____

_____

_____

_____

_____

_____

_____

_____

_____

MESSAGES

Telephone messages

If you need help with grammar, capitalization, or punctuation, refer to the Reference Guide on pages 111–123.

You receive a phone call one afternoon at 3:15. The conversation given on the right takes place.

You:	Hello?
Adam:	Hello. May I please speak to Jake?
You:	I'm sorry, but Jake isn't in. May I take a message?
Adam:	Yes. Tell him Adam called. I was supposed to meet him tomorrow at A-1 Auto Wrecking to get some parts for my car. But I have to work tomorrow, so I won't be able to meet him. Ask him if he can meet me at 4:00 on Thursday afternoon, instead. Oh, and tell him that I heard I could get a better deal at Second Chance Auto Parts at Third and Mission. I'd like to meet Jake there. Tell him to give me a call. I'll be home this afternoon but not after 6:00 tonight. Got all that?
You:	Yes, I think so. Does Jake have your number?
Adam:	I'm sure he does, but just in case, it's 819-5271.
You:	OK. I'll give Jake your message.
Adam:	Thanks. Bye.

Record the message on the form below.

Telephone message for _____

Date _____ Time _____

Caller _____ Phone Number _____

Message _____

_____

_____

_____

_____

_____

Message taken by _____

DIRECTIONS

Road map directions

If you need help with grammar, capitalization, or punctuation, refer to the Reference Guide on pages 111–123.

The paragraph on the right tells where Drake went on Saturday. Read the paragraph and then draw Drake's route on the map below. Choose the route you think would be best. It may help to use a colored pencil.

On Saturday, Drake decided to go to the park with his friends. After he left his house, he stopped at the store. Then he went on to Erin's house. From there, he went to the library to return some books. After that, he stopped at Preston's house. From there, he went to Summit Park.

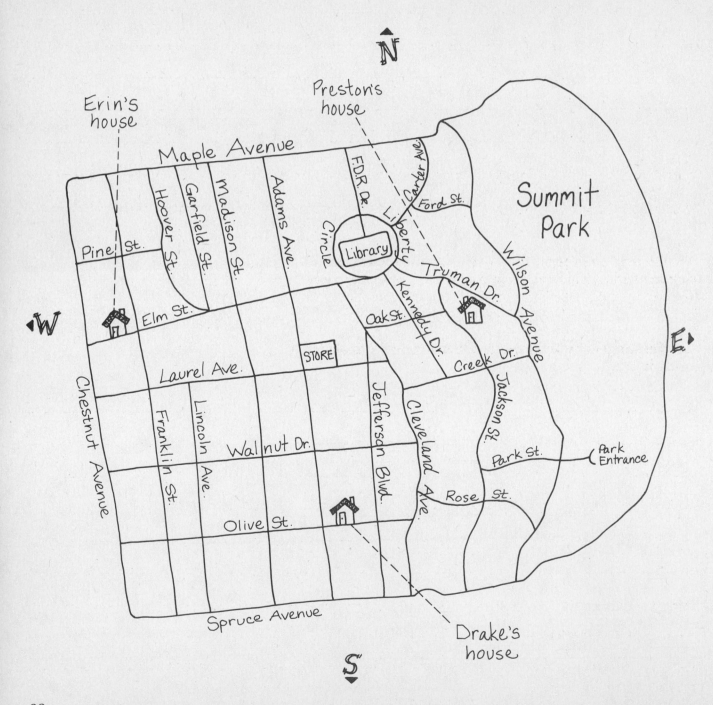

DIRECTIONS
Road map directions

If you need help with grammar, capitalization, or punctuation, refer to the Reference Guide on pages 111–123.

On the lines below, write directions that describe the route Drake took.

_____

_____

_____

_____

_____

_____

_____

_____

On the map on page 98, draw Drake's route home from Summit Park. Assume he didn't make any stops on the way home.

On the lines below, write directions that describe Drake's route home.

_____

_____

_____

_____

_____

_____

_____

_____

INSTRUCTIONS

Instructions for activities

If you need help with grammar, capitalization, or punctuation, refer to the Reference Guide on pages 111–123.

Pick two of the activities given on the right and then write instructions for them on the lines below. Explain *all* the steps. Assume that your reader has no idea what to do.

How to tie a shoelace

How to change the oil in a car

How to make pancakes

How to housebreak a pet

How to buy a car

How to wash clothes

1. _____

_____

_____

_____

_____

_____

_____

_____

2. _____

_____

_____

_____

_____

_____

_____

_____

INSTRUCTIONS

Instructions for activities

If you need help with grammar, capitalization, or punctuation, refer to the Reference Guide on pages 111–123.

Pick two of the activities given on the right and then write instructions for them on the lines below. Explain *all* the steps. Assume that your reader has no idea what to do.

How to choose a pet
How to rent a video movie
How to decide what classes to take
How to name a pet
How to buy clothes
How to prepare for a job interview

1. _____

_____

_____

_____

_____

_____

_____

_____

_____

2. _____

_____

_____

_____

_____

_____

_____

_____

ADVERTISEMENTS

Creating ad copy

If you need help with grammar, capitalization, or punctuation, refer to the Reference Guide on pages 111–123.

Advertisers sometimes use *comparative* and *superlative* forms of adjectives and adverbs. Comparatives often end with **-er.** Superlatives often end with **-est.** For instance, the comparative form of "clean" is "cleaner." It is used when two items are being compared. The superlative form of "clean" is "cleanest." It is used when three or more items are being compared.

Comparatives and superlatives make sense only if it is clear what is being compared to what. An ad might say, "Sudzy Soap gets clothes cleaner!" But cleaner than what? It would be better to say, "Sudzy Soap gets clothes cleaner than Foamy Soap."

A list of products is given on the left below. Select one of the products and write an ad for it on the lines on the right. Aim your ad at children *or* teenagers, and be sure to use comparatives and superlatives correctly.

a breakfast cereal
pizza or hamburgers
a brand of clothing
a stereo system
a particular toy
a soft drink
a movie
a record album
a candy bar

ADVERTISEMENTS

Creating ad copy

If you need help with grammar, capitalization, or punctuation, refer to the Reference Guide on pages 111–123.

Choose two of the products listed on the right. Then, on the lines below, write ads for the products you've selected. Direct your ads toward adults.

a car
a vacation spot
orange juice
a restaurant
a movie
a frozen dinner

1. _____
   _____
   _____
   _____
   _____
   _____
   _____
   _____

2. _____
   _____
   _____
   _____
   _____
   _____
   _____
   _____
   _____

JOURNALISM

News articles

If you need help with grammar, capitalization, or punctuation, refer to the Reference Guide on pages 111–123.

You are a reporter for your local newspaper. You are sent downtown to Fifteenth Avenue and Fulton Street. There you see a man in mountain-climbing gear climbing the city's tallest skyscraper. Make notes of the following information. Use your imagination.

The name of the building: _____

The height of the building: _____

How many people are watching the climb: _____

The climber's name: _____

The age of the climber: _____

A description of the climber: _____

_____

_____

_____

When he started climbing the building: _____

How high he has climbed: _____

His reasons for making the climb: _____

_____

_____

How the climb ends: _____

_____

_____

How the police and city officials feel about the climb: _____

_____

_____

_____

JOURNALISM

News articles

If you need help with grammar, capitalization, or punctuation, refer to the Reference Guide on pages 111–123.

On the lines below, write a news article about the man climbing the skyscraper. Use the notes you have taken to help you write the article.

_____

_____

_____

_____

_____

_____

_____

_____

_____

Movie and TV reviews

Pretend to be the movie reviewer or the television reviewer for your local newspaper. Write either a movie or a television review on the lines below. Assume that your readers haven't seen the movie or TV show you're writing about.

_____

_____

_____

_____

_____

Checkpoint 4

If you need help with grammar, capitalization, or punctuation, refer to the Reference Guide on pages 111–123.

You would like to take your family to visit your uncle, Dr. Frank N. Stein, in Transylvania. On the lines below, write him a friendly letter asking if you may come. Be sure to let your uncle know when you would like to make the visit. Suggest some things you would like to see while you are there. Use the proofreading marks on page 110 to correct your letter.

Your uncle has given you this map to help you find your way from the airport to his house.

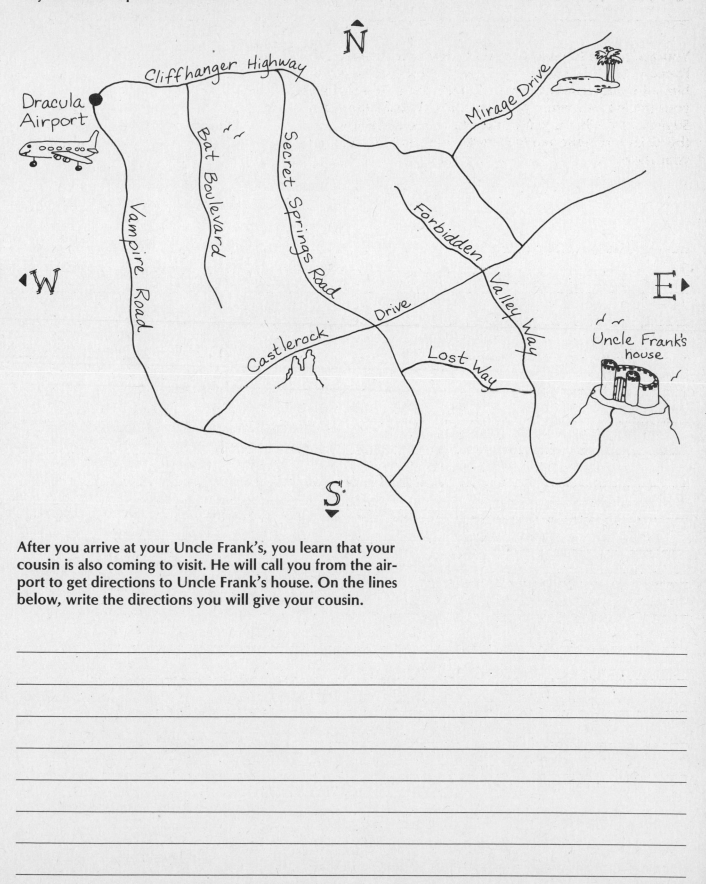

After you arrive at your Uncle Frank's, you learn that your cousin is also coming to visit. He will call you from the airport to get directions to Uncle Frank's house. On the lines below, write the directions you will give your cousin.

_____

_____

_____

_____

_____

_____

_____

_____

At 10:30 one night, you answer the phone for your uncle. The conversation given on the right takes place.

You:	Hello?
Mr. Wolf:	Hello. May I speak to Dr. Stein, please?
You:	He's out for the evening. May I take a message?
Mr. Wolf:	Yes. This is Mr. Wolf at Human Laboratory Supplies. The A-positive blood Dr. Stein ordered is in, but the O-negative blood won't be in for another two weeks. He also asked about discounts on large orders. Tell him that we give discounts of ten percent on orders of five cases or more. If he wants the discount on this order, he'll have to add a case of blood to the order. He might also want to know that a new shipment of shatterproof test tubes has come in. Did you get all that?
You:	Yes, I think so. Should Dr. Stein call you back?
Mr. Wolf:	Only if he wants to order another case of blood so he can get the discount.
You:	OK. What's your number?
Mr. Wolf:	800-1313
You:	I'll give him your message. Good-bye.
Mr. Wolf:	Thank you. Good-bye.

Record the message on the form below.

Telephone message for _____

Date _____ Time _____

Caller _____ Phone Number _____

Message _____

_____

_____

_____

_____

_____

Message taken by _____

Your uncle has been very disturbed lately by the howling of his neighbors' wolves. He writes the letter given on the right to the editor of the Transylvania Digest. He asks you to edit his letter. Use the proofreading marks on page 110 to correct the letter.

Dear Edidor:

    i have ben keept awake awake for the last thre knights bye wolves. My naybores, the Addams family, raise wolves. I dont think the Midnight District of hour town is the rite place for that kind of busines. Besides, the howling upsets my lab experiments. I feel the zoning laws be changed so that wolves cant be razed where peple live and are trying to slep.

                                    Dr. Frank N. Stein

                                    midnight District

Now write a note thanking your uncle for the wonderful visit. Be sure to mention some of the things you especially enjoyed doing while you were in Transylvania.

_____

_____

_____

_____

_____

_____

_____

_____

_____

_____

_____

_____

Proofreading Marks

Mark	Meaning	Example
⊙ or .	Add a period.	Time flies⊙
?	Add a question mark.	How?
!	Add an exclamation point.	They fly too fast!
⋀ or ⸲	Add a comma.	Bozo, however⋀was wrong.
⸏	Reverse the order.	Sue a⸏n Jim were right.
≡	Capitalize the letter.	≡she came late.
/	Make this a small letter.	I'm taking /History.
⌒	Close up this space.	I'm le⌒arning about dead people.
⋀	Add whatever is missing.	Bob took ⋀ᵃclass in cooking.
⸌ or "	Add quotation marks.	Lisa said, "The food here is great. ⸌
⸌ or '	Add an apostrophe.	It⸌s time to fly.
ℓ	Take this out.	I'm not ~~not~~ crazy.
¶	Indent to begin a new paragraph.	¶Every age has its fads. Girls in the 1950s wore poodle skirts.

REFERENCE GUIDE

Grammar Rules

SENTENCES

Grammar 1. Definition of a sentence

A sentence is a group of words that expresses a complete thought. Every sentence must have a subject and a predicate. (See Grammar 3–6.) Every sentence begins with a capital letter and ends with a punctuation mark.

> *That leopard has already killed 400 people.*
> *Is it still hungry?*
> *Be careful!*

Sometimes a sentence may have only one word. (See Grammar 5.)

> *Listen.   Hurry!*

Grammar 2. Kinds of sentences

There are four different kinds of sentences.

A *declarative sentence* makes a statement. A declarative sentence ends with a period.

> *A volcano in the Canary Islands is for sale.*

An *interrogative sentence* asks a question. An interrogative sentence ends with a question mark.

> *Who would want to buy a volcano?*

An *imperative sentence* gives a command. An imperative sentence ends with a period.

> *Show me the list of buyers.*

An *exclamatory sentence* expresses excitement. An exclamatory sentence ends with an exclamation point.

> *They must be crazy!*

Grammar 3. Subjects and predicates in declarative sentences

Every sentence has two main parts, the subject and the predicate. The subject names what the sentence is about. The predicate tells something about the subject.

In most declarative sentences, the subject is the first part. The predicate is the second part.

> *A famous sea captain   was often sick.*
> *He   suffered from seasickness.*

In some declarative sentences, the predicate is the first part. The subject is the second part.

> *Back and forth rolled   the captain's ship.*

Grammar 4. Subjects and predicates in interrogative sentences

Every interrogative sentence has a subject and a predicate. In some interrogative sentences, the subject is the first part. The predicate is the second part.

> *Who   solved the mystery?*
> *Which clue   was most important?*

In most interrogative sentences, part of the predicate comes before the subject. To find the subject and predicate, rearrange the words of the interrogative sentence. Use those words to make a declarative sentence. (The declarative sentence will not always sound natural, but it will help you.) The subject and predicate of the two sentences are the same.

> *Why did   the butler   lie about it?*
> *The butler   did lie about it why?*

Grammar 5. Subjects and predicates in imperative sentences

Only the predicate of an imperative sentence is spoken or written. The subject of the sentence is understood. That subject is always **you.**

> *(You) Try an underhand serve.*
> *(You) Please show me how to do it.*

Grammar 6. Subjects and predicates in exclamatory sentences

Every exclamatory sentence has a subject and a predicate. In most exclamatory sentences, the subject is the first part. The predicate is the second part.

> *Kotzebue Sound, Alaska,   is frozen over nearly all of the time!*

In some exclamatory sentences, part of the predicate comes before the subject.

> *What terrible weather   that city   has!*
> *(That city   has what terrible weather!)*

Grammar 7. Compound subjects in sentences

A sentence with a compound subject has two or more subjects with the same predicate.

> ***Jesse James and his brother Frank** were famous outlaws in the Old West.*
> ***Cole Younger, James Younger, and Robert Younger** were all members of the James gang.*

Grammar 8. Compound predicates in sentences

A sentence with a compound predicate has two or more predicates with the same subject.

> *The postal workers **took in the tailless cat and named him Kojak.***
> *Kojak **lives in the post office, catches mice, and earns a salary.***

Grammar 9. Compound sentences

A compound sentence is made up of two shorter sentences joined by a coordinating conjunction. (See Grammar 45.) A compound sentence has a subject and a predicate followed by another subject and another predicate.

> *G. David Howard set a record in 1978, and it remains unbroken.*
> *Howard told jokes for more than 13 hours, but not all of them were funny.*

NOUNS

Grammar 10. Definition of a noun

A noun is a word that names a person, a place, or a thing.

> *That brave **man** crossed the **ocean** in a **rowboat**.*

Grammar 11. Singular and plural forms of nouns

Almost every noun has two forms. The singular form names one person, place, or thing.

> *Only one **worker** in that **factory** can name the secret **ingredient**.*

The plural form names more than one person, place, or thing.

> *Several **workers** in those two **factories** can name the secret **ingredients**.*

Grammar 12. Spelling plural forms of nouns

For most nouns, add **s** to the singular form to make the plural form.

> *joke—jokes   character—characters*
> *cartoon—cartoons*

If the singular form ends in **s, ss, sh, ch,** or **x**, add **es.**

> *bus—buses   witch—witches*
> *kiss—kisses   fox—foxes*
> *wish—wishes*

If the singular form ends in a consonant and **y**, change the **y** to **i** and add **es.**

> *spy—spies   discovery—discoveries*
> *mystery—mysteries*

If the singular form ends in **f**, usually change the **f** to **v** and add **es.** If the singular form ends in **fe**, usually change the **f** to **v** and add **s.** There are some important exceptions to these rules. Look in a dictionary if you are not sure of the correct plural form.

> *half—halves   wife—wives*
> *loaf—loaves   knife—knives*

Some exceptions:
> *roof—roofs   chief—chiefs   safe—safes*

If the singular form ends in **o**, add **s** to some words and **es** to others. Look in a dictionary if you are not sure of the correct plural form.

> *studio—studios   tomato—tomatoes*
> *piano—pianos   zero—zeroes*

Some nouns change in other ways to make the plural form.

child—children   mouse—mice
woman—women   goose—geese

A few nouns have the same singular form and plural form.

sheep—sheep   deer—deer   moose—moose

Grammar 13. Proper nouns and common nouns

A proper noun is the special name of a particular person, place, or thing. Each word in a proper noun begins with a capital letter.

*Then **Max** stopped in **Junctionville** and ate a **Big Mac**.*

A common noun is the name of any person, place, or thing.

*Then the **man** stopped in a small **town** and ate a **hamburger**.*

Grammar 14. Possessive nouns

The possessive form of a noun shows ownership. Usually the possessive form of a noun is made by adding an apostrophe and **s**. (See Punctuation 20.)

*A **piranha's** teeth are as sharp as razors.*

The possessive form of a plural noun that ends in **s** is made by adding only an apostrophe. (See Punctuation 20.)

*Nobody believed the **explorers'** story.*

Grammar 15. Nouns of address

A noun of address names the person being spoken to. One or two commas separate a noun of address from the rest of a sentence. (See Punctuation 9.)

*Where are you going, **Ricky?***

*I told you, **Lucy,** that I have a rehearsal tonight.*

Grammar 16. Appositive nouns

An appositive noun renames or identifies the noun that comes before it in a sentence. An appositive noun is usually part of a group of words. The whole group of words is called an appositive. One or two commas separate an appositive from the rest of a sentence. (See Punctuation 10.)

*A Ford was the preferred car of John Dillinger, **the famous gangster**.*

*Even his sister, **the president of her own company**, would not hire him.*

VERBS

Grammar 17. Definition of a verb

A verb is a word that expresses action or being.

*The volcano **erupted** suddenly.*

*It **was** a terrific surprise.*

Almost all verbs have different forms to show differences in time.

*Sometimes puffs of smoke **rise** from the volcano.*

*A huge cloud of heavy gray smoke **rose** from it last week.*

Grammar 18. Action verbs

Most verbs are action verbs. An action verb expresses physical action or mental action.

*The committee members **banned** Donald Duck comic books.*

*They **disliked** the duck's behavior.*

Grammar 19. Linking verbs

Some verbs are linking verbs. A linking verb tells what the sentence subject is or is like. The most common linking verb is **be.** (See Grammar 23.)

*A black and white dog **became** a mail carrier in California.*

*The dog's name **was** Dorsey.*

Grammar 20. Verb phrases

A verb phrase is made up of two or more verbs that function together in a sentence. The final verb in a verb phrase is the main verb.

*The 13,000-pound bell **had disappeared**.*

*Somebody **must have stolen** it.*

The verbs before the main verb in a verb phrase are helping verbs. The most common helping verbs are forms of **be (is, are, am, was, were)**, forms of **have (has, have, had)**, and forms of **do (does, do, did)**. (See Grammar 23.)

*That radio station **is sponsoring** a contest.*

*The station **has** already **received** 45,217 postcards.*

Grammar 21. Agreement of verbs with nouns

Verbs that express continuing action or existence and verbs that express current action or existence are in the present tense. Almost all present-tense verbs have two different forms. These two different forms go with different sentence subjects. The verb in a sentence, or the first helping verb in a sentence, must agree with the most important word in the subject of that sentence.

One present-tense form of a verb agrees with singular nouns. This verb form ends with **s.**

> A tick **sucks** blood from larger animals.

The other present-tense form of a verb agrees with plural nouns.

> Ticks **suck** blood from larger animals.

Grammar 22. Agreement of verbs with compound subjects

The present-tense verb form that agrees with plural nouns also agrees with compound subjects. (See Grammar 7.)

> Beth Obermeyer and her daughter Kristen **hold** a record for long-distance tap dancing.

Grammar 23. Forms of the verb *be*

The verb **be** has more forms than other verbs. **Be** has three present-tense forms: **is, are,** and **am. Is** agrees with singular nouns. **Are** agrees with plural nouns. **Am** agrees with the pronoun **I.**

> Mary Lou Retton **is** a famous gymnast.
> Many people **are** her fans.
> I **am** a pretty good gymnast, too.

Most verbs have one past-tense form that tells about action or existence in the past. **Be** has two past-tense forms: **was** and **were. Was** agrees with singular noun subjects. **Were** agrees with plural noun subjects.

> The argument **was** noisy.
> Several neighbors **were** very angry about it.

Grammar 24. Irregular verbs

Usually the past-tense form of a verb ends in **d** or **ed.**

> William Baxter **invented** an important part of the Morse code.

Some verbs change in other ways to form the past tense. These are called *irregular* verbs. Look in a dictionary if you are not sure of the correct past-tense form of a verb.

> Samuel Morse **took** all the credit.

PRONOUNS

Grammar 25. Personal pronouns

A personal pronoun is a word that takes the place of one or more nouns.

> Superman tried to enlist in the Army during World War II, but **he** was found unfit to serve.

Grammar 26. Subject forms and object forms of personal pronouns

Each personal pronoun has a subject form and an object form. These different forms are used in different ways in sentences. (The pronouns **it** and **you** are the same in the subject form and the object form.) These are the subject forms of personal pronouns: **I, you, he, she, it, we, they.** These are the object forms of personal pronouns: **me, you, him, her, it, us, them.**

> **He** saw through a wall and read the wrong eye chart.
> The army did not accept **him.**

Grammar 27. Antecedents of pronouns

A personal pronoun refers to the noun it replaces. That noun is the antecedent of the pronoun.

> **Roy Rogers** became famous in movies. **He** was usually accompanied by his horse, Trigger, and his dog, Bullet.

If a personal pronoun takes the place of two or more nouns, those nouns together are the antecedent of the pronoun.

> **Roy Rogers and Dale Evans** often worked together. **They** made dozens of movies.

Grammar 28. Subject-verb agreement with personal pronouns

The present-tense verb form that agrees with singular nouns also agrees with the pronoun subjects **he, she,** and **it.**

> She **tests** new planes.

The present-tense verb form that agrees with plural nouns also agrees with the pronoun subjects **I, you, we,** and **they.**

> They **test** new planes.

Grammar 29. Indefinite pronouns

A word that refers to a general group but does not have a specific antecedent is an indefinite pronoun.

> ***Nobody*** *can be right about **everything**.*

One common indefinite pronoun, **no one,** is written as two words.

Grammar 30. Subject-verb agreement with indefinite pronouns

The present-tense verb form that agrees with singular nouns also agrees with most indefinite pronouns.

> *Almost everyone **remembers** the Alamo.*
> *No one **knows** exactly what happened there.*
> *Of the accounts written of the battle, several **claim** to be factual.*

Grammar 31. Possessive pronouns

A personal pronoun that shows ownership is a possessive pronoun.

These possessive pronouns are used before nouns in sentences: **my, your, his, her, its, our, their.**

> *Why are **my** gym shoes in **your** locker?*

These possessive pronouns stand alone in sentences: **mine, yours, his, hers, its, ours, theirs.**

> *Are these gym shoes **mine**, or are they **yours**?*

Unlike possessive nouns, possessive pronouns are not written with apostrophes.

Grammar 32. Reflexive pronouns

A pronoun that refers back to a noun or pronoun in the same sentence is a reflexive pronoun. These words are reflexive pronouns: **myself, yourself, himself, herself, itself, ourselves, yourselves, themselves.**

> *The witness had been talking to **himself**.*
> *You should have bought **yourself** a ticket.*

Grammar 33. Demonstrative pronouns

A word that points out one or more people or things is a demonstrative pronoun. These four words can be demonstrative pronouns: **this, that, these,** and **those.**

> ***These*** *are the funniest cartoons.*
> *Nobody laughed at **those**.*

If the word **this, that, these,** or **those** is followed by a noun, the word is not a demonstrative pronoun. (See Grammar 34.)

ADJECTIVES

Grammar 34. Definition of an adjective

A word that adds to the meaning of a noun or pronoun is an adjective. Adjectives usually tell what kind, which one, or how many.

> ***Those exhausted*** *men have been playing tennis for **nine** hours.*

Adjectives that tell what kind can sometimes stand alone.

> *They were **exhausted**.*

Adjectives that tell which one or how many always come before nouns.

> ***Both*** *players have used **several** rackets.*

Grammar 35. The adjectives *a* and *an*

The adjectives **a** and **an** are usually called *indefinite articles.* (The adjective **the** is usually called a *definite article.*) **A** is used before words that begin with consonants or with a "yew" sound.

> ***A*** *penguin cannot fly.*
> *Cooking is **a** useful activity.*

An is used before words that begin with vowels or with an unsounded **h.**

> ***An*** *ostrich cannot fly.*
> *Brutus is **an** honorable man.*

Grammar 36. Predicate adjectives

An adjective that comes after a linking verb and adds to the meaning of the subject noun or pronoun is a predicate adjective.

> *Maria Spelterina must have been **brave**.*
> *Her tightrope walks across Niagara Falls were **dangerous**.*

Grammar 37. Proper adjectives

An adjective that is formed from a proper noun is a proper adjective. Each word in a proper adjective begins with a capital letter.

> *The **American** dollar is worth less than the **British** pound.*
> *The new **Spielberg** film is great!*

Grammar 38. Comparative and superlative forms of adjectives

Adjectives can be used to compare two or more people or things. When only two people or things are compared, use the comparative form of an adjective. To make the comparative form, add **er** to adjectives with one syllable and many adjectives with two syllables. Use **more** (or **less**) before some adjectives with two syllables and all adjectives with more than two syllables. Look in a dictionary if you are not sure of the correct comparative form of an adjective.

> *Buster Keaton was **funnier** than Charlie Chaplin.*
> *Buster Keaton was **more amusing** than Charlie Chaplin.*

When more than two people or things are compared, use the superlative form of an adjective. To make the superlative form, add **est** to adjectives with one syllable and many adjectives with two syllables. Use **most** (or **least**) before some adjectives with two syllables and all adjectives with more than two syllables. Look in a dictionary if you are not sure of the correct superlative form of an adjective.

> *Buster Keaton was the **funniest** movie actor who ever lived.*
> *Buster Keaton was the **most amusing** movie actor who ever lived.*

The comparative and superlative forms of the adjective **good** are **better** and **best**.

> *Buster Keaton was a **better** actor than Charlie Chaplin.*
> *Buster Keaton was the **best** movie actor who ever lived.*

The comparative and superlative forms of the adjective **bad** are **worse** and **worst**.

> *The Revenge of the Killer Tomatoes was a **worse** movie than The Fly.*
> *The Revenge of the Killer Tomatoes was probably the **worst** movie ever made.*

ADVERBS

Grammar 39. Definition of an adverb

A word that adds to the meaning of a verb or verb phrase is an adverb. Adverbs usually tell where, when, how, or how often.

> *The rodeo rider **bravely** mounted the mustang **again**.*

Grammar 40. Comparative and superlative forms of adverbs

Adverbs can be used to compare the actions of two or more people or things.

When only two people or things are compared, use the comparative form of an adverb. To make the comparative form, usually use **more** (or **less**) before the adverb. Add **er** to a few short adverbs.

> *Polly speaks **more clearly** than that other parrot.*
> *Polly can fly **higher** than that other parrot.*

When more than two people or things are compared, use the superlative form of an adverb. To make the superlative form, usually use **most** (or **least**) before the adverb. Add **est** to a few short adverbs.

> *Of all those parrots, Polly speaks **most clearly**.*
> *Of all those parrots, Polly can fly **highest**.*

The comparative and superlative forms of the adverb **well** are **better** and **best**.

> *That parrot behaved **better** than your pet cat.*
> *Of all the unusual pets in the show, the parrot behaved **best**.*

The comparative and superlative forms of the adverb **badly** are **worse** and **worst**.

> *Your pet monkey behaved **worse** than that parrot.*
> *Of all the unusual pets in the show, your cat behaved **worst**.*

Grammar 41. Using adjectives and adverbs

Use an adjective to add to the meaning of a noun or a pronoun.

> *The **proud** actor accepted the prize.*

Use an adverb to add to the meaning of a verb or a verb phrase. Many (but not all) adverbs end in **ly**.

> *The actor accepted the prize **proudly**.*

Grammar 42. The adverb *not*

The adverb **not** changes the meaning of the verb or verb phrase in a sentence.

> *The soldiers in the fort would **not** surrender.*
> *Help did **not** arrive in time.*

Grammar 43. Avoiding double negatives

The adverb **not** is a negative word. Other common negative words are **no, never, no one, nobody, nothing, nowhere, hardly, barely,** and **scarcely.** Use only one negative word to make a sentence mean **no** or **not.**

> ***No one** ever understands how I feel.*
> *My friends **never** understand how I feel.*
> ***Hardly** anyone understands how I feel.*

Grammar 44. Adverbs used as intensifiers

Certain adverbs add to the meaning of adjectives or other adverbs. These special adverbs are sometimes called *intensifiers*.

> One **terribly** nosy neighbor heard the whole conversation.
>
> **Very** nervously, she told the police all about it.

CONJUNCTIONS

Grammar 45. Coordinating conjunctions

A word used to join two equal parts of a sentence is a coordinating conjunction. The most common coordinating conjunctions are **and, but,** and **or.**

> Many people have driven across the country, **but** these two men did it the hard way.
>
> Charles Creighton **and** James Hargis drove across the country **and** back again.
>
> They never stopped the engine **or** took the car out of reverse gear.

Grammar 46. Subordinating conjunctions and complex sentences

A word used to begin an adverb clause is a subordinating conjunction. The most common subordinating conjunctions are listed below.

after	before	though	when
although	if	unless	whenever
because	since	until	while

An adverb clause is a group of words that has a subject and a predicate but that cannot stand alone as a sentence. An adverb clause functions like an adverb. It tells when, where, how, or why. An adverb clause usually comes at the end or at the beginning of a sentence. (See Punctuation 8.) A sentence formed from an adverb clause (which cannot stand alone) and a main clause (which can stand alone) is called a *complex sentence*.

> Otto E. Funk played his violin **while he walked from New York City to San Francisco.**
>
> **When he finished his musical journey,** both his feet and his hands were tired.
>
> **Whenever it is threatened,** an opossum plays dead.
>
> It can be poked, picked up, and even rolled over **while it remains completely rigid.**

INTERJECTIONS

Grammar 47. Definition of an interjection

A word that simply expresses emotion is an interjection. A comma or an exclamation point separates an interjection from the rest of a sentence. (See Punctuation 11.)

> **Oh,** now it makes sense.
>
> **Wow!** That's terrific news!

PREPOSITIONS

Grammar 48. Definition of a preposition

A word that shows the relationship of a noun or pronoun to some other word in a sentence is a preposition. The most common prepositions are listed below.

about	below	in	to
above	beneath	into	toward
across	beside	like	under
after	between	of	until
against	beyond	off	up
along	by	on	upon
among	down	over	with
around	during	past	within
at	except	since	without
before	for	through	
behind	from	throughout	

Grammar 49. Prepositional phrases

A preposition must be followed by a noun or a pronoun. The preposition and the noun or pronoun that follows it form a prepositional phrase.

> A new record **for sit-ups** was set **by Dr. David G. Jones.**
>
> His family and friends were very proud **of him.**

Often, other words come between the preposition and the noun or pronoun. Those words are also part of the prepositional phrase.

> He set a new record **for consecutive straight-legged sit-ups.**

Grammar 50. Objects of prepositions

A preposition must be followed by a noun or a pronoun. That noun or pronoun is the object of the preposition.

> One of the main **characters** of **Star Trek** didn't appear until the second **season.**

Grammar 51. Personal pronouns in prepositional phrases

A personal pronoun that is the object of a preposition should be in the object form. These are object-form pronouns: **me, you, him, her, it, us, them.**

*The other presents for **her** are still on the table.*

*The most interesting present is from **me**.*

Grammar 52. Prepositional phrases used as adjectives

Some prepositional phrases are used as adjectives. They add to the meaning of a noun or pronoun in a sentence.

*The Caribbean island **of Martinique** is a department **of the French government**.*

Grammar 53. Prepositional phrases used as adverbs

Some prepositional phrases are used as adverbs. They add to the meaning of the verb or verb phrase in a sentence.

***In 1763**, Napoleon Bonaparte's wife, Josephine, was born **on Martinique**.*

SENTENCE PARTS

Grammar 54. Simple subjects

The most important noun or pronoun in the subject of a sentence is the simple subject of that sentence. The object of a preposition cannot be the simple subject of a sentence.

*A 27-year-old **man** from Oklahoma   swam the entire length of the Mississippi River.*

***He**   spent a total of 742 hours in the river.*

Grammar 55. Simple predicates

The verb or verb phrase of a sentence is the simple predicate of that sentence.

*Actor W. C. Fields   **may have had** 700 separate savings accounts.*

*Fields   **used** a different name for each account.*

Grammar 56. Direct objects

A word that tells who or what receives the action of a verb is the direct object of the verb. A direct object must be a noun or a pronoun. A personal pronoun that is a direct object should be in the object form. These are object-form pronouns: **me, you, him, her, it, us, them.**

*The first aspirin tablets contained **heroin**.*

*A German company sold **them** for 12 years.*

Grammar 57. Indirect objects

A word that tells to whom (or what) or for whom (or what) something is done is the indirect object of the verb expressing the action. An indirect object comes before a direct object and is not part of a prepositional phrase. An indirect object must be a noun or a pronoun. A personal pronoun that is a direct object should be in the object form. These are object-form pronouns: **me, you, him, her, it, us, them.**

*Professor Sommers gave his **students** the same lecture every year.*

*He told **them** a familiar story.*

Grammar 58. Predicate nominatives

A word that follows a linking verb and renames the sentence subject is the predicate nominative of a sentence. A predicate nominative must be a noun or a pronoun. A personal pronoun that is a predicate nominative should be in the subject form. These are subject-form pronouns: **I, you, he, she, it, we, they.**

*The best candidate was **Andrea**.*

*In my opinion, the winner should have been **she**.*

Capitalization Rules

Capitalization 1.   First word in a sentence

Begin the first word in every sentence with a capital letter.

> *Who won the eating contest?*
> *That man ate 17 bananas in two minutes.*

Capitalization 2.   Personal pronoun *I*

Write the pronoun **I** with a capital letter.

> *At the last possible minute, I changed my mind.*

Capitalization 3.   Names and initials of people

Almost always, begin each part of a person's name with a capital letter.

> *Toby Ohara   Rosie Delancy*
> *Sue Ellen Macmillan*

Some names have more than one capital letter. Other names have parts that are not capitalized. Check the correct way to write each person's name. (Look in a reference book, or ask the person.)

> *Tim O'Hara   Tony de la Cruz*
> *Jeannie McIntyre*

Use a capital letter to write an initial that is part of a person's name.

> *B. J. Gallardo   J. Kelly Hunt*
> *John F. Kennedy*

Capitalization 4.   Titles of people

Begin the title before a person's name with a capital letter.

> *Mr. Sam Yee   Captain Cook*
> *Dr. Watson   Governor Maxine Smart*

Do not use a capital letter if this kind of word is not used before a person's name.

> *Did you call the doctor?*
> *Who will be our state's next governor?*

Capitalization 5.   Names of relatives

A word like **grandma** or **uncle** may be used as a person's name or as part of a person's name. Begin this kind of word with a capital letter.

> *Only Dad and Aunt Ellie understand it.*

Usually, if a possessive pronoun comes before a word like **grandma** or **uncle,** do not begin that word with a capital letter.

> *Only my dad and my aunt understand it.*

Capitalization 6.   Names of days

Begin the name of a day with a capital letter.

> *Most people don't have to work on Saturday or Sunday.*

Capitalization 7.   Names of months

Begin the name of a month with a capital letter.

> *At the equator, the hottest months are March and September.*

Capitalization 8.   Names of holidays

Begin each important word in the name of a holiday with a capital letter. Words like **the** and **of** do not begin with capital letters.

> *They usually have a picnic on the Fourth of July and a fancy dinner party on Thanksgiving.*

Capitalization 9.   Names of streets and highways

Begin each word in the name of a street or highway with a capital letter.

> *Why is Lombard Street known as the most crooked road in the world?*

Capitalization 10.   Names of cities and towns

Begin each word in the name of a city or town with a capital letter.

> *In 1957, the Dodgers moved from Brooklyn to Los Angeles.*

Capitalization 11.   Names of states, countries, and continents

Begin each word in the name of a state, country, or continent with a capital letter.

> *The story was set in Nevada, but they shot the film in Mexico.*
> *There are very high mountain peaks in Antarctica.*

Capitalization 12. Names of mountains and bodies of water

Begin each word in the name of a mountain, river, lake, or ocean with a capital letter.

*Amelia Earhart's plane was lost somewhere over the **Pacific Ocean**.*

Capitalization 13. Abbreviations

If the word would begin with a capital letter, begin the abbreviation with a capital letter.

*On the scrap of paper, the victim had written, "**Wed.—Dr. Lau.**"*

Capitalization 14. Titles of works

Use a capital letter to begin the first word, the last word, and every main word in the title of a work. The words **the, a,** and **an** do not begin with capital letters except at the beginning of a title. Coordinating conjunctions and prepositions also do not begin with capital letters. (See Grammar 45 and Grammar 48.)

*Archie and Edith were the main characters in the television series **All in the Family**.*

Capitalization 15. Other proper nouns

Begin each major word in a proper noun with a capital letter. A proper noun is the special name of a particular person, place, or thing. (See Grammar 13.) Usually, the words **the, a,** and **an,** coordinating conjunctions, and prepositions do not begin with capital letters. (See Grammar 45 and Grammar 48.)

*Jerry rushed to the **Burger King** and ordered three **Whoppers**.*

Capitalization 16. Proper adjectives

Begin each word in a proper adjective with a capital letter. A proper adjective is an adjective that is formed from a proper noun. (See Grammar 37.)

*That **American** author writes about **English** detectives.*
*She loves **Alfred Hitchcock** movies.*

Capitalization 17. Direct quotations

Begin the first word in a direct quotation with a capital letter. (See Punctuation 14–16.)

*Dr. Pavlik said, "**There** are simply no teeth in the denture law."*

If the words that tell who is speaking come in the middle of a quoted sentence, do not begin the second part of the quotation with a capital letter.

*"**There** are simply no teeth," said Dr. Pavlik, "**in** the denture law."*

Capitalization 18. Greetings and closings in letters

Begin the first word in the greeting of a letter with a capital letter.

__Dear__ Mr. Lincoln: __Dear__ Uncle Abe,

Begin the first or only word in the closing of a letter with a capital letter.

__Sincerely__ yours,   __Very__ truly yours,
__Love__,

Capitalization 19. Outlines

In an outline, begin the first word of each heading with a capital letter.

II. Houses by mail order
  A. First sold by Sears, Roebuck in 1903
    1. Build-it-yourself kits
    2. Included all materials and instructions
  B. Other companies now in business

In an outline, use capital Roman numerals to label main ideas. Use capital letters to label supporting ideas. For ideas under supporting ideas, use Arabic numerals. For details, use small letters. Use a period after each Roman numeral, capital letter, Arabic numeral, or small letter.

I. Miner George Warren
  A. Risked his share of Copper Queen mine in bet
    1. Bet on race against George Atkins
      a. Warren on foot
      b. Atkins on horseback
    2. Lost property worth $20 million

Punctuation Rules

Punctuation 1. Periods, question marks, and exclamation points at the ends of sentences

Use a period, a question mark, or an exclamation point at the end of every sentence. Do not use more than one of these marks at the end of a sentence. For example, do not use both a question mark and an exclamation point, or do not use two exclamation points.

Use a period at the end of a declarative sentence (a sentence that makes a statement).

A hockey player must be able to skate backward at top speed.

Also use a period at the end of an imperative sentence (a sentence that gives a command).

Keep your eye on the puck.

Use a question mark at the end of an interrogative sentence (a sentence that asks a question).

Who is the goalie for their team?

Use an exclamation point at the end of an exclamatory sentence (a sentence that expresses excitement).

That was a terrific block!

Punctuation 2. Periods with abbreviations

Use a period at the end of each part of an abbreviation.

Most titles used before people's names are abbreviations. These abbreviations may be used in formal writing. (**Miss** is not an abbreviation and does not end with a period.)

Dr. Blackwell   *Mr. Bill Tilden*
Ms. Maureen Connolly

Most other abbreviations may be used in addresses, notes, and informal writing. They should not be used in formal writing.

Lake View Blvd.   *Mon. and Thurs.*
Fifth Ave.   *Dec. 24*

Do not use periods in the abbreviations of names of government agencies, labor unions, and certain other organizations.

Tomorrow night CBS will broadcast a special program about the FBI.

Do not use periods after two-letter state abbreviations in addresses. This special kind of abbreviation has two capital letters and no period. Use these abbreviations only in addresses.

Their new address is 1887 West Third Street, Los Angeles, CA 90048.

Punctuation 3. Periods after initials

Use a period after an initial that is part of a person's name.

Chester A. Arthur   *C. C. Pyle*
Susan B. Anthony

Punctuation 4. Commas in dates

Use a comma between the number of the day and the number of the year in a date.

Hank Aaron hit his record-breaking home run on April 8, 1974.

If the date does not come at the end of a sentence, use another comma after the number of the year.

April 8, 1974, was an exciting day for Hank Aaron's fans.

Do not use a comma in a date that has only the name of a month and the number of a year.

Aaron hit his final home run in July 1976.

Do not use a comma in a date that has only the name of a month and the number of a day.

April 8 is the anniversary of Aaron's record-breaking home run.

Punctuation 5. Commas in place names

Use a comma between the name of a city or town and the name of a state or country.

The world's largest chocolate factory is in Hershey, Pennsylvania.

If the two names do not come at the end of a sentence, use another comma after the name of the state or country.

Hershey, Pennsylvania, is the home of the world's largest chocolate factory.

Punctuation 6. Commas in compound sentences

Use a comma before the conjunction—**and, but,** or **or**—in a compound sentence. (See Grammar 9 and Grammar 45.)

Eighteen people tried, **but** *no one succeeded.*

Punctuation 7. Commas in series

Three or more words or groups of words used the same way in a sentence form a series. Use commas to separate the words or word groups in a series.

Jamie, Mitch, Kim, Lou, and Pablo *entered the contest.*

Each contestant **swam one mile, bicycled two miles, and ran five miles.**

Punctuation 8. Commas after introductory phrases and clauses

Use a comma after a phrase that comes before the subject of a sentence. A phrase is a group of words that usually functions as an adjective or an adverb. One kind of phrase is a prepositional phrase. (See Grammar 49.)

In the old dresser, *Penny found the diamonds.*

If the entire predicate comes before the subject of the sentence, do not use a comma. (See Grammar 3.)

In the old dresser lay the diamonds.

Use a comma after an adverb clause at the beginning of a sentence. (See Grammar 46.)

When he was first named hockey's most valuable player, *Wayne Gretzky was only 18 years old.*

Punctuation 9. Commas with nouns of address

Use a comma after a noun of address at the beginning of a sentence. (See Grammar 15.)

Fernando, *that was a terrific pitch!*

Use a comma before a noun of address at the end of a sentence.

That was a terrific pitch, **Fernando!**

If a noun of address comes in the middle of a sentence, use one comma before the noun and another comma after it.

That, **Fernando,** *was a terrific pitch!*

Punctuation 10. Commas with appositives

Use a comma before an appositive at the end of a sentence. (See Grammar 16.)

This costume was worn by George Reeves, **Hollywood's first Superman.**

If an appositive comes in the middle of a sentence, use one comma before the appositive and another comma after it.

George Reeves, **Hollywood's first Superman,** *wore this costume.*

Punctuation 11. Commas or exclamation points with interjections

Usually, use a comma after an interjection. (See Grammar 47.)

Well, *we should probably think about it.*

Use an exclamation point after an interjection that expresses excitement.

Wow! *That's a terrific idea!*

Punctuation 12. Commas after greetings in friendly letters

Use a comma after the greeting in a friendly letter.

Dear John,   Dear Uncle Theodore,

Punctuation 13. Commas after closings in friendly letters and business letters

Use a comma after the closing in a letter.

Love,   Yours sincerely,

Punctuation 14. Quotation marks with direct quotations

A direct quotation tells the exact words a person said. Use quotation marks at the beginning and at the end of each part of a direct quotation.

"Look!" cried Tina. "That cat is smiling!"

"Of course," said Tom. "It's a Cheshire cat."

Punctuation 15. Commas with direct quotations

Usually, use a comma to separate the words of a direct quotation from the words that tell who is speaking. (See Punctuation 16.)

Jay asked, "Who won the game last night?"

"The Cubs won it," said Linda, "in 14 innings."

Punctuation 16. End punctuation with direct quotations

At the end of a direct quotation, use a period, a comma, a question mark, or an exclamation point before the closing quotation marks.

If the direct quotation makes a statement or gives a command at the end of a sentence, use a period.

> *Linda said, "The Cubs won last night's game."*
> *Jay said, "Tell us about the game."*

If the direct quotation makes a statement or gives a command before the end of a sentence, use a comma.

> *"The Cubs won last night's game," said Linda.*
> *"Tell us about the game," Jay said.*

If the direct quotation asks a question, use a question mark.

> *"Was it an exciting game?" asked Jay.*

If the direct quotation expresses excitement, use an exclamation point.

> *Linda yelled, "It was great!"*

Punctuation 17. Quotation marks with titles of works

Use quotation marks around the title of a story, poem, song, essay, or chapter.

> **"Happy Birthday to You"** *is the most popular song in the world.*

If a period or a comma comes after the title, put the period or comma inside the closing quotation mark.

> *The most popular song in the world is* **"Happy Birthday to You."**

Punctuation 18. Underlines with titles of works

Underline the title of a book, play, magazine, movie, television series, or newspaper.

> *One of the best movies about baseball was* **The Natural.**

Punctuation 19. Apostrophes in contractions

Use an apostrophe in place of the missing letter or letters in a contraction.

> *is not—isn't   Mel is—Mel's   I will—I'll*

Punctuation 20. Apostrophes in possessive nouns

Use an apostrophe and **s** to write the possessive form of a singular noun. (See Grammar 14.)

> *This cage belongs to one bird. It is the* **bird's** *cage.*
> *This cage belongs to Tweeter. It is* **Tweeter's** *cage.*

Use only an apostrophe to write the possessive form of a plural noun that ends in **s.**

> *This is a club for boys. It is a* **boys'** *club.*

Use an apostrophe and **s** to write the possessive form of a plural noun that does not end in **s.**

> *This is a club for men. It is a* **men's** *club.*

Punctuation 21. Colons after greetings in business letters

Use a colon after the greeting in a business letter.

> *Dear Mrs. Huan: Dear Sir or Madam:*
> *Dear Senator Rayburn:*

Punctuation 22. Colons in expressions of time

When you use numerals to write time, use a colon between the hour and the minutes.

> *5:45 P.M.   9:00 A.M.   12:17 P.M.*

Punctuation 23. Hyphens in numbers and fractions

Use a hyphen in a compound number from twenty-one to ninety-nine.

> *thirty-seven   fifty-eight   seventy-three*

Use a hyphen in a fraction.

> *one-quarter   two-thirds   seven-eighths*